BURGUNDY

Burgundy

THE COUNTRY, THE WINES, THE PEOPLE

EUNICE FRIED

Photographs by Susan Oristaglio
and Eunice Fried

A Cornelia & Michael Bessie Book

HARPER & ROW, PUBLISHERS, New York
Cambridge, Philadelphia, San Francisco, London
Mexico City, São Paulo, Singapore, Sydney

FIRST EDITION

Designer: Sidney Feinberg

Library of Congress Cataloging-in-Publication Data

Fried, Eunice.
  Burgundy : the country, the wines, the people.

  "A Cornelia & Michael Bessie book."
  Includes index.
   1. Burgundy (France)—Social life and customs.
2. Burgundy (France)—Description and travel.
3. Country life—France—Burgundy. 4. Wine and wine
making—France—Burgundy. I. Title.
DC611.B7742F75   1986   944'.4   85-45193
ISBN 0-06-039049-2

86 87 88 89 90 MPC 10 9 8 7 6 5 4 3 2 1

TO S.B.G.

CONTENTS

[*vii*]

CONTENTS

LIST OF ILLUSTRATIONS

ACKNOWLEDGMENTS

With deep gratitude, I thank:

Jean-Michel Lafond, who opened the door to Cîteaux.

Mary Lyons, who counted the barrels of France.

Rory Callahan, who knows how to prune a vine in every language.

Kenneth Onish, who worked with Frank Schoonmaker and knows everyone else who did.

Doris Tobias, who made a visit of the mind to Vieux Moulin's kitchen.

Natalie Petouhoff, who offered nimble typing fingers and kind words.

Marie Ponzo, who was, as always, friend, support and careful reader.

Julian Bach, an early believer and sustaining guide.

Cornelia and Michael Bessie, my editors, for their unbeatable combination of patience, intelligence and love of Burgundy.

And to Rebecca Wasserman, who made all things possible.

BURGUNDY

PROLOGUE

✼

There is a tiny village in the wine region of Burgundy that grows no grapes and makes no wine. It is on a road to nowhere particular, a village outside of time that is little more than a collection of centuries-old stone houses and barns notched deeply into a narrow valley. On the east side of the valley, thickly wooded slopes rise over 200 feet before limestone cliffs curve out in a bold flange that juts up nearly another 200 feet. On the west, the valley is braced by steep green grazing fields punctuated with outcroppings of rock, squared by fences and topped with clusters of trees.

The village is Bouilland, and it has 134 people. It also has cows, sheep, horses, chickens, geese, goats, rabbits, cats and dogs. But since the schoolteacher retired and became the village mayor, it has no school. Since the baker retired, it has no bakery. There is no butcher, no doctor, no pharmacy, no post office. And while it has a church, an eleventh-century structure of stones that squats on a hillside, it has no priest and depends instead on the curé who travels from village to village, caring for each hamlet's spiritual needs.

Bouilland is ten miles from Beaune, the wine center of Burgundy. From that walled town, the road leads northwest through the wine village of Savigny-lès-Beaune along Route D2.

Past Savigny-lès-Beaune, the vineyards end, and the road twists through land of a different texture. On the right, the banks rise sharply to forests where logs waiting to be hauled to Bouilland's fireplaces are stacked against the backs of tree trunks to keep them from rolling down. To the left, through a lacy-leafed curtain, the land dips to the meandering Rhoin River, a silver thread of a stream, and to pastures where white Charolais cattle, France's prized source of beef, graze. At the far end of the pastures, the terrain rises again to a forest so thick that the treetops intertwine.

Six miles past Savigny-lès-Beaune, a small road sign reads "Bouilland." The area surrounding the village has a strong Roman history, and stones and foundations of Roman encampments can still be found, although few people seek them out. More come to visit the ruins of the Abbey of Saint Marguerite, which thrived from the eleventh to the sixteenth century, and to hike and climb along the cliffs.

Still, no crowds are drawn to Bouilland, and the center of the tiny village would have virtually no visitors if it weren't for two attractions that evolved only a few years ago. One is the Hostellerie du Vieux Moulin, which had its beginning in the last century as a mill and has been reborn under a new young chef-owner as the most exciting restaurant in Burgundy.

The other reason to go to Bouilland is the one that first lured me. As a wine writer, I had been to Burgundy many times. But Bouilland has no vineyards; it is not even a way station between vineyards. And until 1981, I had not been there. That year when I was in Burgundy, I went to Bouilland to interview a woman whose story intrigued me. I wrote an article about her, but long after the article had been published, the woman, her farm, the village and, radiating out from Bouilland, the life, the traditions, every part of Burgundy, whether it dealt directly with winemaking or not, stayed with me. There was more "story" than one, two, a dozen articles could contain.

The woman is Rebecca Wasserman. Early in 1984, I returned to Burgundy and stayed on her farm in Bouilland for much of the next year. In that time, I found a Burgundy not conveyed through vintage charts and vineyard lists. I lived in a rustic country full of grace and vigor. I drank wines as sensuous as liquid silk. I met people who are as much a part of the land as the vines and stones and oak trees are.

Burgundy takes hold of you and does not let you go.

1

REBECCA WASSERMAN

The entrance to the farm in Bouilland where Rebecca Wasserman lives is through old iron gates that as long as I've known her have never been closed. They open onto the courtyard, and as I drove through them, Becky came out to greet me, a slight woman barely five feet tall, peering through big, round eyeglasses, and smiling.

"Welcome to Bouilland," she said, offering a hand, as fine-boned as a child's. As she stood there, a mass of dark, curly hair falling to her shoulders, she was warm and gracious and poised. And despite an innate shyness and a whisper of hesitancy that surfaced, as weightless as cobwebs, at moments, she was clearly mistress of her farm, her business, her life.

Those fleeting moments were the only hints of her earlier life. In all other ways, her manner reflected the person she is now, a woman who, barely a decade ago, when she noted her direction, took measure of it and turned it around. Today she is a formidable success—as a wine broker, barrel broker, innovator, entrepreneur.

In this most French of France's wine regions, Rebecca Wasserman was the first American wine broker to live in Burgundy and operate directly from the source of her product. And in a region dominated by large *négociant*-shippers, she is one of the few brokers dealing primarily with grower-producers who bottle their own wine. She runs her businesses on an international scale, and she does it all from an old farm in an isolated little village in the heart of Burgundy.

When Becky welcomed me to Bouilland, her gesture seemed to embrace all of the valley. But in fact, she was speaking of her Bouilland, her farm, the property that had begun in a small way in the 1400s. As it grew, so did the number and size of its buildings. By the 1700s, all the structures that are standing today had been completed. The original small barn had become L-shaped, with the large addition stretching back more than sixty feet. Across the courtyard, a house almost as long as the barn had been built.

Behind the house, past the vegetable and flower gardens, a shed for rabbits, a cote where pigeons were once raised for eating and a bread oven that is still functioning were erected, low, small buildings with worn, flat stone roofs that look like hats whose feathers had long ago drooped. Beyond them, a second, slightly longer barn was added.

All were constructed of local stones, and, it has been said, the stones of some of the later buildings, like those of other barns and houses in Bouilland, came from the ruins of the Abbey of Saint Marguerite.

In France, Becky told me, it is the custom to name country fields rather than to number them. And on Becky's farm, what remains of the original land today covers about twenty acres and is composed of two separate fields. One is Le Serbet; the other is La Couture Sous La Pierre Chaude.

"What does La Couture Sous La Pierre Chaude mean? You could say 'the seam under the hot rock,' and it might be that once there was a hot spring that ran under a rock. But no one is sure. Certainly, we're not aware of any hot springs on the property, and we have no especially large rock. It's really not translatable; it's a name."

After decades of disuse, the farm is active again. Paul Gutigny, the farmer, comes early each morning to care for the sheep, goats, rabbits, chicken and geese, and the vegetable and flower gardens. But the farm's agricultural aim today is simply to be self-sufficient; it does not rely on its products for income.

Instead, the main barn has been converted to the home in which Becky lives, and part of the old house has become the office of Le Serbet, Becky's wine brokerage, named after the farm's major field.

Rebecca Wasserman at home on her farm in Bouilland.

Becky is an intense woman whose thoughts seem to race quickly through her mind and across her face. She brims over with expressive intelligence, and she gives subtle hints of a vivid inner life, and flashes, too, of an affective imagination. And when she says, "I want no limits put on me other than those I put on myself," you have only to think of her accomplishments and you believe her.

Since the early nineteenth century, much of Burgundy's wines have been sold through the *négociants*. They buy most of their wine from small growers, usually blend together those wines that come from the same vineyard appellation and sell the wine under the *négociant*'s name.

In contrast, most of the producers with whom Becky Wasserman deals are estate bottlers. Some of them may own no more than ten to fifteen acres, but they make their wine, they age it and they bottle it to be sold under their own name.

Becky began in 1976 as a broker of oak barrels in which wine is aged. She made her first move into wine brokering when, on a visit to California for her barrel business, she was asked to look for some good Burgundies made by small producers.

Four years later, she formalized her two brokerage businesses as S.A.R.L. (Société à Responsabilité Limité) Le Serbet. In French law, S.A.R.L. is a limited corporation that must begin with a minimum of 20,000 francs (currently, about $2,500).

A small sum of money with which to start a business. But at the beginning, hers was a small business. Le Serbet began in a tiny office in Beaune with a staff that consisted of Becky and a secretary, a short list of wine suppliers and one client, an importer in northern California. And for a while, Le Serbet remained small.

In those days, few wine importers understood Burgundy's small grower-producers. They knew the names of the big and famous *négociant*-shippers. They were the old names traditionally associated with Burgundy, and for decades nearly the only Burgundy names found in most wineshops. Importers did not know the people with whom Becky worked. Her suppliers were winemakers who produced perhaps a few thousand cases of wine, and many of them had never shipped beyond Europe or, in some instances, beyond France.

Nor did the importers know Becky Wasserman. Who, they asked, is this novice on the wine scene, this woman with the quick smile and encyclopedic knowledge of Burgundy's wines, a shy woman who sells wine with articulate passion? Why was she, an American, working with French wine? Why was she living in France? And how, after all, did she get there?

2

FROM BIRTH TO BURGUNDY

Becky was born Rebecca Rand in New York City on January 18, 1937, the only child of a stockbroker and a Hungarian ballerina. Life began with private schools and maids, but the accoutrements of wealth disappeared in the later 1940s, "because my father's firm just never recovered from the effects of the war," Becky says.

From private school, she switched to public school, Hunter College High School, and then, on a scholarship, she attended Bryn Mawr College for a year.

Soon after she left school, at eighteen, she married; and for six years, until they were divorced, she and her young husband lived in Cambridge, Massachusetts, and Philadelphia.

After the marriage ended, Becky stayed on in Philadelphia studying composition and the piano, which she had played since she was six. One day, as she was leaving her music teacher's studio, she met the student whose lesson came after hers, a tall, broad-shouldered young artist named Bart Wasserman. On March 17, 1962, about a year after their meeting, they were married.

Their first son, Peter, was born two years later. When he was a year old, the three Wassermans and Becky's mother (her father had died in 1964) traveled to France. For Yolanda Rand, who was born in Europe and had had a career there as a dancer, returning to the Continent was a kind of homecoming. For Becky, who had never been to Europe, it was a matter of "falling in love immediately, totally, with France."

They returned to Philadelphia after the summer, but while all of France remained a good memory, it was Burgundy especially that burned bright.

In 1967, the Wassermans returned to spend the summer in that fabled wine region. Barely two hundred miles southeast of Paris, Burgundy is centuries away from it in spirit. Burgundy is the essence of wine country, all vineyards and old villages and deep wine cellars, with days of misty white fog and other days of gold and silver light.

"It was glorious, a summer of splendid weather. I was enchanted—with the architecture, the wine, the food. Everything Burgundian," Becky said. So enchanted, in fact, that before the summer was over, she and Bart decided to move there permanently.

"Since our first trip, two years before," Becky remembers, "when I first saw the little villages, the well-tended vegetable gardens, I wanted only to come back to France."

Still—why Burgundy?

"I probably won't really know the answer for years."

During the summer of 1967, the Wassermans drove through the villages of Burgundy looking for property. "When we saw a place we liked, we would stop and ask if it was for sale. I suppose that was naive of us," Becky said. They asked the realtors of the region. They asked friends. It was nearly the end of the summer before they heard about the farm in Bouilland.

The big barn that is now the house had its original walls, but the floor was earth, there were stone feeding troughs under a hayloft at one end of the barn, and the remnants of pig sties under the hayloft at the other end. What is now a bucolic green lawn between the horse field and the sheep field was covered with nettles. The property, which had ceased to be a working farm thirty or more years earlier, was owned by Mademoiselle Alphonsine Serrigny, a woman then in her early seventies, and she did not want to sell it.

Many of the village people had asked to buy it, Mademoiselle Serrigny said—not for the house, not for living there or for restoring it, but for the pastures. Bouilland, after all, is an agricultural and dairy village, and pastures are valuable assets. But she had said no to them. She did not want to sell. That is, until she met Bart Wasserman. "With his artist's sense, Bart seemed to be able to envision the farm as it had been, and an immediate rapport sprang up between them," Becky recalled. " 'What do you want to do with it?' Mademoiselle Serrigny asked him. He told her he wanted to take it back to what it had been, to make it live again."

The response decided the farm's fate. The day before the Wassermans left to return to the United States, they signed an agreement with Mademoiselle Serrigny to buy the property. The conditions included a clause that guaranteed Mademoiselle's right to live on the property for the rest of her life (she has since moved to a nursing home), and specified that the Wassermans pay half the price in cash, the rest in monthly payments.

The Wassermans sold their home in Philadelphia, and in 1968 they moved to Burgundy, a rural world, rustic and traditional and wrapped securely in its medieval heritage.

The farm in Bouilland was then still years away from being habitable.

While it was being renovated, the Wassermans lived in a house in Saint-Romain, a small wine village south of the town of Beaune. The house was square and white and, Becky says, "slightly run down." But it was large enough for Becky and Bart, for Peter, for Paul, who had been born in 1966, and for Becky's mother, who had taken an apartment in Beaune and spent weekends with the Wassermans in Saint-Romain.

A small, elegant woman, Yolanda Rand was known to everyone as Granny, and even the French, usually formal and proper with strangers, quickly took to greeting her with *"Bonjour,* Granny," and *"Comment ça va,* Granny?"

The Wassermans' house was next to the one-room school that Peter and Paul would attend. And it was at an angle with a little country inn named Hôtel des Roches, after the cliffs that border Saint-Romain on two sides. The hotel had no bathtubs. But the Wassermans' house did. Gilbert Lefèvre, the owner of the hotel, observed the Wassermans. They were friendly people, no? They were hospitable, no? He asked to have a meeting with them; he had a most delicate subject to discuss. He realized this might be perhaps a bit forward, but would Monsieur and Madame mind if once in a while he sent a few of his guests—only the most important, the most impeccable people, of course—to the Wasserman home for a bath?

Did the Wassermans mind? "Not at all," Becky said. "We got to know the most interesting people that way. In fact, that's how we met Michael Foot, who later became leader of Great Britain's Labor party; his wife came over to take a bath."

It was a very busy, frustrating, fascinating and, in many ways, amusing time, Becky says of their life in Saint-Romain. "Bart, a contemporary artist, had his work to set up. I had the household to set up." There were the problems of a different culture. And there were the pleasures. "It seemed everyone we knew in the United States came to see us. We had a wonderful cook—Madame Jeanne Rondet. And we were meeting all sorts of people in Burgundy."

Her first trip to a Burgundian wine cellar was to the one owned by Roland Thévenin, then mayor of Saint-Romain.

"I didn't know the rituals yet. I didn't know you're supposed to spit, not swallow, the wine when you taste in a cellar. So I swallowed—everything. I wobbled up the cellar stairs feeling something was terribly wrong but too light-headed to know what it was.

"From there, the wine experience grew very intense. We met René Mugneret, who invited us to his cellar in Vosne-Romanée and to the festival of Saint Vincent—he's the patron saint of wine." It was at the festival that the Wassermans met Philippe de Magenta, who owns the wine estate Domaine du Duc de Magenta, with vineyards along the Côte de Beaune.

Soon after they settled into Saint-Romain, Bart Wasserman began to put together a wine cellar. He amassed a collection that was to become renowned in Burgundy, and from the beginning, the quality of his cellar and his ability to taste brought many wine people into their lives. Hubert de Montille of Volnay. Jacques Seysses of Domaine Dujac in Morey-Saint-Denis. Gérard Potel of Pousse d'Or in Volnay. Anthony Hanson, a young Englishman then working in the wine trade in Burgundy, and his wife, Rosemary.

It was during this time, too, that the Wassermans met Aubert de Villaine, whose family owns half of Domaine de la Romanée-Conti in Vosne-Romanée. It was also during this time that Becky, who had always had a great interest in cooking, became more and more deeply involved with French food. Aubert had not yet married Pamela Fairbanks, and the three of them—Aubert, Bart and Becky—struck up a close friendship. They tasted wine together. They went to Burgundy's restaurants together. Becky cooked for Bart and Aubert. Granny mended for Aubert. And all through this time, still more people came to visit. "Aubert loved that house and family and their easy bohemian way of life," Pamela Fairbanks de Villaine told me.

Becky, too, remembers those days with affection. She remembers waking each morning to the sound of hammering as the coopers across the road made oak barrels. Tonnellerie François Frères, with its insistent, measured, early-morning beat. It was a part of Saint-Romain's life, and it became part of her life as well.

She remembers sitting in front of the Hôtel des Roches, looking around at the school, the *tonnellerie,* the vineyards, the cliffs, and saying to herself over and over, "I am living in a Burgundian village. I'm living in a Burgundian village," unable to believe in her good fortune.

"I look back now, and know we were probably our happiest in Saint-Romain."

3

THE BARN—A RE-CREATION

As soon as the Wasserman family had settled in Saint-Romain, Bart began the restoration of the farm in Bouilland. The main barn, a huge L-shaped mass of old stones, had to be converted into a home for the family, and in the second barn, an artist's studio had to be created.

For nearly four years, he drove from Saint-Romain to Bouilland almost daily. He did much of the labor himself. He found, sometimes with great difficulty, the right artisans to execute his ideas—carpenters and woodworkers and stonemasons. He traveled throughout Burgundy, looking and studying and assimilating the architectural history of the region.

The main barn opened onto the courtyard, but the other side, facing south to the valley, was a solid wall of stone. Bart Wasserman added windows and doors, placing them to allow exactly the right amount of light to enter. He measured the glass panes of the Musée Rolin in Autun, the great medieval center about thirty miles southwest of Beaune, and used those measurements for the windows and doors of the barn. He examined doors at the Hôtel-Dieu, the famous fifteenth-century hospice in Beaune, and from them he designed the interior doors of the barn. The original part of the barn, which had been built in the 1400s, became the kitchen. At that end, where the main part of the barn joins the oldest section, he removed the cattle-feeding trough and made the space into a dining room. Above it, what had been a hayloft became a balcony overlooking the center of the house.

In the style of old Burgundian barns, there was a hayloft at the other end of the barn as well. In that space, he constructed bedrooms for the family. Below, where there had once been pigsties, he made two more bedrooms, for guests.

He had an interior stone wall taken apart and reconstructed about ten feet farther away from the center of the barn, forming the inner wall of the bedroom area. In that wall a fireplace was built, with a bend formed into the chimney that catches the eye and pulls it up, up to where the chimney pushes through the roof.

He found a carpenter who took the oak of an old winepress and fashioned it into a staircase leading to the family bedrooms at one end of the barn and another staircase leading to the balcony at the other end.

In the center of the house, there emerged a vast room, more than 28 feet long and 26 feet wide, its ceiling soaring 29½ feet to the rafters. On the bare earth floor Bart Wasserman put in *dalles,* broad, flat flagstones like those found on the floors of old cathedrals. These *dalles* were from Comblanchien, a marble quarry about ten miles north of Bouilland, and he searched them out in old Burgundian farms and chapels. He looked especially for those with soft pink and yellow and beige casts to them, removed them himself and carted them back to the farm in Bouilland. He spaced them on the floor so close together that they needed no joining.

The beams in the barn were sanded by hand. In places where wood had to be replaced, Bart found old oak and soaked it in a solution of lime to age it to the color and texture of the original wood.

It had taken eight months from the time the Wassermans reached an agreement with Mademoiselle Serrigny until the transaction was completed. It took six times as long to restore the crumbling old barn and to construct a studio in the second barn. Bart Wasserman saw that every part of the work was handcrafted, and he insisted on perfection.

He began in 1968. On July 8, 1972, the family moved from Saint-Romain to Bouilland, into a home that was a perfect balance of stone and oak, of space and light, with the most subtle nuances of color.

Thirteen years later, Becky was to look around the magnificent house and remark that every day she lived there, she discovered something new.

"Really, isn't that one of the attributes of great art?"

The entrance to Rebecca Wasserman's farm in Bouilland.

4

COUNTRY LIVING

Bouilland was an isolated valley, but it was not a lonely one. There was the glory of the land and the luxury of space. There was the need to settle in, the need to rejuvenate the farm. There was so much to be done, and at the beginning, at least, there was a splendid excitement.

"I remember the first gardens," Becky said. "Bart laid them out, and they looked like land art—rows of lettuces, banks of sweet peas, onions and sweet corn. And our first jams. We made them of raspberries, plums and cassis. We made chutney, as well. At the first pig killing, the butcher who was making *boudin* from the blood had me taste the raw mixture before putting it into the sausage casings. He was testing me in a way, and I passed instead of passing out."

"Peter and Paul went to the one-room schoolhouse here. Henri Robert was their teacher. He's the mayor now."

On a chilly evening, years after those early days in Bouilland, Becky looked back, gathering together memories like fragments of old possessions to hold in the palm of her hand. But even as she tried to feel them one by one, they seemed to spill over, cascading in a stream of recollections.

"I remember the first two sheep we bought. One of them produced three lambs. Since she could only nurse two at a time, we made a temporary manger in our dining room for the extra one, and we all took turns bottle feeding him for three weeks. We named him Mr. Mustard.

"When there were flowers in the garden, Bart would make

immense bouquets for the living room and dining room—wonderful masses of color that happened to be made of flowers. In those days, Volnay First Growths cost only seven, eight francs a bottle, less than two dollars, and Bart served them lavishly. I cooked. I loved to cook then. So many people came by for an apéritif, a meal, a weekend, a year. They came from Burgundy, from all over France, England, the United States, Australia, New Zealand.

"By the time we moved into the farm, a lot of people knew about Bart's cellar, and we knew many people in the wine trade. Aubert and Pamela de Villaine were here often. Anthony and Rosemary Hanson visited. Steven Spurrier, the Englishman who started L'Académie du Vin, the wine school in Paris, came in 1972. A year later, he brought Jon Winroth. Jon lives in Paris and was co-founder of L'Académie. He was also writing the wine column for the *International Herald Tribune* then."

On this evening, the great stone room was quiet except for the crackle of burning logs. Becky smoked as she talked, flicking the ashes toward the fireplace. A small figure in sweater and pants. One moment she was nestled into a large armchair, another moment she stood at the fireplace, her back to it, resting her hands on the tops of the andirons.

Becky has a lovely voice and a remarkable way of using it. Each word is distinct and precise, and at the same time the tone is soft, the expression eloquent, the feeling passionate. A fine crystal bell with a delicate echo.

"Bart and the people who came to visit had high standards for wine, and they rarely varied from those standards. There were always long discussions about wine, about every nuance in a wine. They would talk about such things as how long a particular wine had been left in cask before bottling. Should it have been left longer? Had it been left too long?"

Bart Wasserman's wines were kept in a stone cellar in the second barn. The collection continued to grow, and visitors continued to come. "One year," Peter Wasserman told me, "we counted 413 guests."

What the guests saw and enjoyed was a kind of *mise en scène,* a bit of magic that the Wassermans made for them. And they continued to make magic even after they discovered that while the house, the wine cellar, the guests, were the stuff of dreams, maintaining the farm was a grim reality. "In retrospect," Becky says, "I can see that moving from Saint-Romain to Bouilland was far more traumatic than moving from Philadelphia to France.

"In Saint-Romain we had the normal complexities of adjusting to a new culture. In Bouilland we had the monumental responsibility of the property. I grew up in a city. I was not equipped to deal with country living. Bart wanted to be in his studio making his art, but instead he had to direct everybody and everything—the local help, friends who wanted to help, the three buildings, the garden, twenty acres, the animals. I was hopeless at judging rural priorities.

"There were wonderful quiet moments, certainly," Becky added, "when I was busy in the kitchen and Bart was working in his studio, and I would have the most extraordinary feeling of peace."

But even the moments of peace became tinged with a sense of misgiving, Becky says. "For all that Burgundy had to offer in terms of landscape, light and architecture, it could not fulfill a contemporary artist. It was a lovely place to live, but it was becoming a lonely place for Bart to work."

For Becky, too, there were troubling moments that went beyond the problems of managing a rural estate. There was the growing awareness that she was a totally dependent woman. And she also began to question her role as the obliging hostess always on call. There were times guests would go off to visit domaines and Becky wanted to go with them, but they would leave their children with her. "You don't mind, Becky, do you?" they'd say. Becky said no, she didn't. But she was beginning to mind terribly.

There was the time when she was cleaning up after a dinner party, and one of the guests said to her, "You wash wineglasses better than anyone I've ever known."

"I almost threw the glasses at him," she says. "He meant it as a compliment, but all I could think was, What kind of epitaph would that make?"

She didn't throw the glasses at him, but she did begin to look more deeply into herself. She knew she did not want to be known as an A-one baby-sitter and glass-washer. She began, tentatively at first, to read more about wine. She began to go along with Bart more often when he went tasting. There were more visits to vintners, more talks with them. Burgundy is perhaps the most difficult wine region to know, a tiny region that through the chance of history and geography is divided into small patchwork squares and rectangles of vineyards, each differing from the other often by only the most subtle nuance. It was these nuances that Becky tried to learn and identify.

Yet for all her efforts, she says, she remembers feeling she could not keep up the pace. "There were so many pieces—the house, the farm, the family, the guests. I often felt that the only things I was doing successfully were cooking and playing the harpsichord. I felt incompetent. I didn't drive a car in those days. I had to rely on others if I wanted to go to Beaune or, for that matter, anyplace outside of Bouilland."

Early in 1975, a California winemaker visiting Burgundy told the Wassermans he wanted to buy oak barrels. Bart introduced him to Jean François the cooper, their former neighbor in Saint-Romain. The winemaker bought the barrels but failed to pay for them. That summer, Becky and her sons went to the United States. She wanted to show Peter and Paul the country where they were born, and she hoped to collect the money owed the cooper. It was her first visit to the vineyards of California.

"I met so many people, especially in Napa Valley. And it was so beautiful there. As much as I love Burgundy, I will never forget sitting in front of the Joseph Phelps Vineyards and thinking, what a spacious, happy landscape. I had gone there with Philip Diamond, an attorney in San Francisco who wanted to start a wine importing business. It was he who introduced me to Bruce Neyers, who works at the Phelps winery, and his wife, Barbara. The Neyerses were so extraordinarily kind to me. It was before my barrel business began, but they were almost like parents to that business, in the way they supported and encouraged me."

There was other encouragement too. "When people heard I was from Burgundy and knew a cooper, many of them suggested I start a barrel business. But I just brushed it aside."

After California, the three Wassermans traveled to Yellowstone National Park. On their last night in one of the lodges in the park, the manager, who had become acquainted with Becky and had heard about her cooking skills, told her his cook had just left. Would she like to take the job and stay on at Yellowstone?

"I sat up all night, thinking. If I could produce a respectable *boeuf Bourguignon* in Burgundy, why couldn't I make buffalo stew in Yellowstone? It had been a long, long time since I'd been offered a job with a salary, and it came at a time when I felt very despondent about my ability—or rather, lack of ability—to run the farm successfully. I remember very clearly every thought of that night. I remembered something I should never have forgotten: that almost all the women in my family did things—my mother ran a ballet school when I was a child, when there was no economic necessity for it; my great-grandmother had been the first woman granted a degree in surgery in Vienna. I realized, too, that so many of the women I had met in California worked. They did something that was theirs alone. I began to understand in a way I hadn't before how important it was for a woman to do things on her own, to be financially independent. Most of all, that night, I kept thinking that someone had offered me a job. I was employable. It gave me a new confidence."

In the morning, Becky refused the job. "When I left Yellowstone," she said, "my ideas for the future were only half—no, less than half—formulated. But it seems to me now, looking back, that all the seeds were sown on that trip, and things began coming together in my mind even before I realized it."

About a month after Becky returned to Burgundy, Jean Francois asked her to sell barrels for him in the United States. She had a contact—Bruce Neyers. She had talked about his barrels when she was in California. She might be the right person for the job, he felt.

Since her visit to Yellowstone, Becky had often wondered how she could take the things she knew—food, wine, music, for example—and turn something of them into a kind of work. "I was a great admirer of cottage industries like Laura Ashley's, and I began to think, What could I do to set up my own little business in Burgundy?"

Barrels were not among the things she felt she knew. Still, with Jean François's offer, her thoughts began to take shape. Bart encouraged her to try it, and Becky could see the possibilities. Early in 1976, she took her first independent business trip—to California to sell barrels.

"I quickly realized I didn't know enough about barrels or the relationship between wine and wood to be effective. I also didn't know how to sell. And to make matters worse—you know I smoke, and my sample barrel reeked of cigarette smoke."

But good things came of the trip. She visited Philip Diamond, who had begun to organize his importing business; through Philip, she met Mel Knox, who was the wine buyer for a wine and cheese shop in San Francisco.

When she returned to Burgundy, Becky began to study cooperage seriously, and at the same time she plunged still more deeply into her study of wine.

Meanwhile, Bart Wasserman left Burgundy for four months to set up a studio in New York.

"Bart missed contact with the art world. He's a totally committed artist, but in Burgundy he was admired for other things —for his house, gardens, bouquets, wine. He had no audience for his art. People here didn't understand nonfigurative painting. The de Villaines were the only people in Burgundy who were involved with his work. Anthony and Rosemary Hanson, who were living in London by then, collected Bart's art. But for many of our guests, a visit to Bart's studio was uncomfortable. When they looked at his paintings, they didn't know how to respond. Where were the trees, the apples, the nudes? Jon Winroth was one of the rare visitors who always asked to visit the studio. He understood that the house and the cellar existed because Bart was an artist."

Becky now had her driver's license, which, in her eyes, "made all things possible." She continued to learn more about wine and barrels. And her desire to create her own small business in Burgundy became keener.

"I felt so strongly the need for financial independence. I felt it was so important for me as a woman. I was beginning at last to see that I really could become a businesswoman."

In her barrel-selling trip to California, Becky had met André Tchelistcheff, the legendary Russian-born winemaker who had been with Beaulieu Vineyards in Napa Valley for thirty-five years. He was planning to take a group of California winemakers to Europe on a tour, and Becky had invited him to come by Bouilland when the group was in Burgundy. He did—with thirty-eight people. "We cooked for days. I asked everyone I knew who was bilingual. We borrowed all the chairs from the Bouilland schoolhouse. In all, we had about sixty people. Besides André, Louis Martini was there, and so were Bob and Noni Travis of Mayacamas Vineyards in Napa."

Soon after the group returned to California, Becky received her first order for barrels, from Mayacamas. She drove over to the cooperage in Saint-Roman and dashed out of the car calling to Robert François, Jean's father: "The first order—I've got my first order for barrels!"

"How many?" he asked.

"Fifteen barrels! Fifteen barrels!"

"Fifteen barrels?" He shrugged.

5

OF OAK TREES

AND BARRELS

The square white house where Becky Wasserman once lived in Saint-Romain is still there. And so are the one-room schoolhouse and the Hôtel des Roches, although Gilbert Lefèvre has long ago retired. But the *tonnellerie* across the road where the pounding of the cooper's hammer wakened Becky each morning is silent now, used only to house finished barrels trucked up from the newer, larger cooperage that was built in 1981 on the rim of the village.

When I arrived in Saint-Romain on an April morning, every door was shut against the chill. I was to meet the cooper, Jean François, but in a village without street names, without numbers, I could not be sure which house was his. A sharp right, he had said, up a steep hill, a white house on the left. So I took a sharp right and drove up a hill. And there I saw the only person outdoors in Saint-Romain, an elderly woman walking along in felt slippers.

"Pardon, Madame, do you know where Jean François the cooper lives?"

"*The* Jean François?" she answered. "You mean Jean François the mayor. Come, I'll show you."

I parked the car and we walked to the house across the narrow road, Madame leading the way, felt slippers flapping, up a flight of stairs. She opened the door and there was Jean François, tall and lean, with well-muscled arms and a shock of graying hair—barrelmaker and, since 1976, mayor of Saint-Romain's 340 inhabitants.

"Ah, I see you've met my mother," he said.

Within a half hour, Jean François and I left to drive to the oak forests 125 miles west-southwest of Saint-Romain. Wearing a sports jacket, an open-necked shirt and a jaunty scarf, he maneuvered his Mercedes-Benz around curves like the auto racer he had wanted to be some twenty years earlier. Instead of following a career on the fast track, he had followed his father into the family's barrelmaking business, Tonnellerie François Frères. The *tonnellerie* was begun three generations ago in the early 1940s by Jean's grandfather. Jean's father and uncle joined the cooperage after the war; hence the name *frères*, or brothers. Jean's uncle died young, and his father, Robert, continued alone. In the early 1970s, Robert made Jean, his only son, head of François Frères. Robert François died in 1978.

Under Jean's direction and through Becky's and later Mel Knox's work as brokers in the United States, the *tonnellerie* has grown from one whose business had been limited chiefly to Burgundy to one with a sizable international market. Jean François now has an annual production of 7,500 *fûts* or *tonneaux*, as barrels are generally called in France, just as "cask" and "barrel" are used interchangeably in the United States. Nearly all of them are the traditional Burgundy barrel, called a *pièce*, which holds 228 liters (about sixty American gallons). The François production accounts for about a third of all casks with a capacity of 225 to 450 liters produced in Burgundy and makes François Frères the largest single *tonnellerie* in the region. And it accounts for 6 percent of the 121,000 casks in that size range made throughout France each year. Jean François sells about half of his barrels in France, where his clients include Domaine de la Romanée-Conti and the Hospices de Beaune. The rest are exported to the United States, Italy, Switzerland and Australia.

On this overcast day, we drove to the department of Nièvre, where the oak forests of Nevers are found. While more than thirty kinds of wood have been used over the centuries to make barrels, white oak is the wood of choice in which to age fine wines. It is a hard wood that can produce tight barrels; it is resilient, allowing it to be bent to shape; and it has a high tannin content, which, among other assets, helps to make the wood resistant to decay.

More than four hundred species of oak grow in the world. In France, most wine barrels are made from *Quercus robur* or *Quercus pedunculata.* While it is said that *Quercus robur,* whose acorns are attached directly to the tree branch, prefers drier, higher regions and *Quercus pedunculata,* whose acorns grow on a stem emanating from the branch, generally favors deep, moist soils, actually both species are often found in the same forests. In fact, only a few forests are planted exclusively—or almost exclusively—in one or the other.

One of those is the great forest of Bertranges in the region of Nièvre, where almost all the oaks are *Quercus robur,* although the region itself is abundant in *Quercus pedunculata.*

Most of Jean François's wood comes from Bertranges, but he also buys oak from France's other forests. He buys from Tronçais in the department of Allier, where because the trees grow extremely tall and slim, the grain is extremely fine. He buys from Limousin in the department of Haut-Vienne near the city of Limoges, where because the oaks are planted farther apart and grow thicker in girth than the trees in Tronçais, their grain is wider and coarser. He buys, too, from the Vosges in eastern France; and in small quantity from Burgundy, mostly from the forests of Cîteaux, east of Nuits-Saint-Georges.

"An oak should be at least fifty centimeters thick before it is cut," Jean François said. "But in Bertranges, even a one-hundred-fifty-year-old tree is not necessarily very big."

Jean François drove through the labyrinthine forest of Bertranges, a vast, dense, ghostly-silent woodland; then out across the gently rolling countryside to a *chantier de fente de merrain,* a lumberyard where the oak logs are split first into quarters and then into *merrains,* or rough staves. In a large open shed, we stepped over oak in every phase of its way to being part of a barrel, through chippings and past screeching hydraulic machines. The wood is split along the natural grain; no fine barrel is made of sawed wood.

The *chantier* belonged to Denis Charlois. A barrel-chested man in his early forties, he is the fifth generation of his family to be a *fendeur,* or wood splitter, and he talks about oaks as other people talk about their children. He picked up a log that had been quartered. "We cannot use the sap wood, this outer portion. And we cannot use this center core. It is only the part between, the middle part, that can be turned into staves for a wine barrel."

How do you judge a good tree? How do you know when it is ready to be cut? He shrugged. "I know. That's all. I know when it's ready."

But how? Is it the height? The shape? The color of the trunk?

"No, you tell a tree's age by its thickness. I look for a straight tree with no branches on the trunk. That would make knots in the wood, and it could not be used for barrel staves. Even on the most perfect tree, the only part we can use for staves is a few meters of the trunk; it could be from as little as one meter to as much as six meters if it is a very tall, very beautiful tree. Still, generally, only a quarter of a tree can be made into staves. We lose the rest."

Fendeurs cut down their oaks between October and February, when the trees have less sap and are less porous. And within these months, Jean François says, they cut them *"en vieille lune,* at the time of the old moon, when the sap does not flow at all." And what is the time of the "old moon"? "Those few days when there is *no* moon."

From Denis Charlois's *chantier,* we visited Jean François's other supplier of Bertranges oak—Raymond Fuseau, one of the few *fendeurs* who still split logs into *merrains* completely by hand. He works alone in a small open shed, slicing his logs with his ax, along the wood's natural grain, which runs parallel with the radius of the tree. Nearby, he keeps a small fire going by tossing in the splinters that fly as he cuts his logs. Beyond the fire is a pile of whole raw logs waiting to be split and contoured into barrel staves.

"The distance between age rings in oaks averages about one centimeter," Monsieur Fuseau said. "And the oaks we cut in the forests of Bertranges measure about 140 to 160 centimeters in circumference." That is about all he said. Accustomed to long days working alone, he tugged his cap, picked up his ax and returned to his solitary splitting.

Like many of France's oak forests, Bertranges is owned by the state and operated by the government's O.N.F., or Office

Jean François at his cooperage in Saint-Romain.

National des Forêts. It is O.N.F. that makes all decisions regarding forests, even such small details as where to place the paths leading in and out of them. Every year, O.N.F. publishes a booklet listing the parcels of each forest that are ready to be cut, and then auctions the right to cut these parcels to private persons.

The bulging cylindrical wooden container we know as a barrel had an indefinite birth date. Certainly, containers made of wood were known at least as far back as the Egyptians, but they were straight-sided and were used for dry products, such as the corn measure represented in the tomb of Hesi-Re, from about 2800 B.C. Constructed of separate planks of wood with beveled edges, it was carefully fitted and held together by three hoops of bent wood.

To ferment and store wine, however, the Egyptians used amphorae. Made of clay, these vessels were used by many Mediterranean people over the centuries. They came in a variety of shapes and sizes, but all had similar characteristics: an oval body, a narrow bottom, often ending in a knob that served as a third handle when pouring from it, an elongated neck, two handles that rose almost to the mouth, and a mouth narrow enough to be easily sealed.

The Greeks fermented their wine in large, flat-bottomed clay jars called *pithoi.* They would then draw wine off from the *pithoi* into amphorae. For a time, the Romans, too, used amphorae for wine and, like the Greeks, for oil, water and other liquids, as well.

According to the Roman historian Pliny the Elder, who lived in the first century A.D., the craft of barrelmaking as we know it was invented in Europe by the inhabitants of the Alpine valleys. The first European barrels evidently date from the Late Bronze Age in what is now Switzerland. The ensuing Iron Age brought finer tools to the early coopers. And by the time the barrel made its way to the Roman world, just before the beginning of the Christian era, it had developed into a rather fine specimen, with a bulge, staves and metal hoops.

When the Greek writer Stabo mentioned "wooden *pithoi"* in

A worker at the cooperage fitting staves into an iron hoop.

the last decades before Christ, he noted that these early barrels were made by the Celts, who smeared the cracks between the staves with pitch in order to make them leakproof.

Today, pitch is not needed to produce a leakproof barrel. But in most ways, the cooper's art has not changed radically. While machines are used to simplify or refine or improve some phases of the process, barrelmaking is still primarily a handcraft.

When the *merrains* arrive at Tonnellerie François Frères in Saint-Romain, they are stacked outdoors in an open pattern so that air can circulate between the layers, and allowed to remain there in the rain, the sun, the heat and cold. The rains wash away some of the excess tannins and other harsh components. Outdoors, the wood dries slowly, uniformly, contracting evenly.

After the wood has been aged, usually for eighteen to twenty-four months, it is brought indoors to the *tonnellerie,* where it undergoes a series of preparatory steps. First, each rough stave is cut, most often to a length of 90 to 95 centimeters (approximately 3 feet), depending on the client's specifications. Its sides are tapered slightly at the ends, making them narrower than the middle of the stave so that they fit together snugly when the barrel is curved into shape. The flat part of the stave that will form the inside of the finished barrel is hollowed out very slightly. The staves are then planed and loaded onto a *gabarit,* a flat frame whose width holds exactly enough staves to make one barrel. The staves are not of uniform width because each has been cut to follow its natural grain, and so the number needed to make one barrel varies. Generally, it takes twenty-seven or twenty-eight staves to form one Burgundy *pièce.*

A worker takes a width of staves on the *gabarit* and, standing up one stave at a time, fits it carefully and snugly next to the previous one within an iron hoop, to form a circle. When he has used a width of staves, he has completed the circle. He then slips another temporary iron hoop around the staves, just above the first hoop, and a new barrel, called a *coque* at this early stage, has begun to take shape. It is ready for the first fire.

A cooper's fires are small and low, contained within a grate on the ground and fed sometimes with wood scraps, sometimes

Barrels heating over fires.

by gas. The fledgling barrel is placed over the fire to heat slowly and, thus, evenly. Too hot a fire, and the wood will crack.

The first fire warms the staves for a few minutes. When the barrel is transferred to the second and main fire, a cable is put around the end that has no iron hoops. Gradually, as the wood heats, the worker tightens the cable, drawing the staves closer together, a process called *cintrage.*

When the staves have been pulled in as far as the worker feels is needed, he adds two iron hoops and removes the cable. With four temporary hoops in place, the barrel receives its third and last fire for a few minutes. It now has its shape—a bulging middle, called the bilge, and narrower ends. As it cools, the curve in the wood sets.

A skillful *tonnelier* uses only as much heat as the barrel needs to be bent to the proper curvature. Some clients, however, want more of a toast on the inside of their barrels. To achieve this, the barrels are left on each fire for a minute or two longer, depending on the degree of toast specified, and on the *tonnelier.*

Next, the barrel is trimmed and its ends are reamed on the inside. The temporary iron hoops are removed and replaced with permanent ones: four, six or eight, depending on the client's order. Galvanized hoops are added for exports; hoops painted black are used for barrels sold in France.

The flat ends of each barrel—called *les fonds*—are made individually for each barrel and fit into the *croze,* or groove, at each end. The hoops are pushed down to their final position by a hydraulic machine because, Jean François says, "this is one job where a machine does it better. It is very difficult to do properly with only human strength."

The barrel is scraped and sanded. A few liters of cold water are poured into the barrel and air pressure is added. The barrel is rocked and rolled to check for leaks. If it is deemed leakproof, it is taken to the old *tonnellerie* in the village, where it stays until it is shipped to the client. To make that one barrel required ten workers at the cooperage as well as Jean François and, long before, the wood splitter.

Jean François will also fill orders for Bordeaux-style barrels, which are called *barriques* and require slightly longer, thinner staves. But most of his production is composed of the traditional

Burgundy *pièce.* Somewhat shorter in length and broader at the bulge than the *barrique,* the *pièce* is made of thicker staves and the finished barrel has a more pronounced curvature. Despite the minor differences in their physical appearances, both the Burgundy *pièce* and the Bordeaux *barrique* have about the same capacity, sixty American gallons, with the Bordeaux barrel usually holding two to three liters less. As well as *pièces* and *barriques,* Tonnellerie François Frères makes barrels of other dimensions to order, beginning with those that hold as little as ten liters.

There are about a dozen *tonnelleries* in the Côte d'Or. Most are small, operating with one or two coopers and an assistant. But there is also one sizable cooperative, formed in the late 1960s by five coopers, which exports under the name Les Tonnelleries de Bourgogne. Although the cooperative now consists of three *tonneliers,* the export name remains the same. Within Burgundy, however, each *tonnelier* sells barrels under his own name. They are Gaston Billon, head of the cooperative, Jacques Damy and Roger Rémond. No *tonnellerie* by itself approaches the size of Jean François's production.

Whatever the size of the *tonnelleries,* the craft of the cooper remains the same. It is one forged millennia ago, which, with only a few refinements along the way, continues pretty much as it began.

Modern science has found better methods of fighting vine diseases. New inventions have offered better ways of controlling fermentation temperatures and other aspects of winemaking. But in more than two thousand years, no one has found a better way to age fine wine than in a well-made oak barrel.

6

BUILDING THE BROKERAGE

Becky studied oaks and forests and barrels, reading everything she could find on the subjects. "But it was only when I went to the forest for the first time that I began to understand what I had studied. And every time I've been back, every time I've been to the cooperage, I've found something new to see and wonder about."

By the time Mayacamas gave Becky her first order, she had learned the basics of her subject. Now there was the business of the brokerage.

French oak barrels first came to California in the 1960s. Martin Ray in Santa Clara County and Hanzell Vineyards, a small winery in Sonoma County, imported the first few; Robert Mondavi and Louis Martini of Napa Valley were the first to import them in sizable quantity. In 1965, Richard Graff, co-owner of Chalone Vineyard in the benchlands of the Gavilan Mountains in Monterey County, ordered fifty barrels from Tonnellerie Sirugue in Burgundy for his 1966 vintage.

Within a year, Dick Graff became the agent for Sirugue barrels in the United States. He issued a catalog and set no minimum on the number of barrels a winery could purchase. Business expanded, and soon he was handling barrels from Demptos in Bordeaux as well as barrels from Italy and Germany. It was Graff who first insisted that barrels imported into the United States be made with galvanized hoops. "I knew American winemakers would never put up with rusting iron hoops," he says.

Orders for Burgundy barrels increased so rapidly that Sirugue could not keep up with them. To alleviate the problem, Monsieur Sirugue helped organize the cooperative Les Tonnelleries de Bourgogne, which included four coopers besides himself. Eventually, Monsieur Sirugue pulled out of the cooperative and returned to exporting his barrels individually. So did Henri Meyer. Dick Graff became more involved with Chalone; in 1974, he decided to leave the barrel business and concentrate wholly on the winery. As he let go of his suppliers, others in California became their agents. It was soon after that Becky became a barrel broker for François Frères.

"I came to the business so naive that I wasn't able to understand why certain things couldn't happen." And because she could not see limits, her business grew quickly.

"We made it very easy for a small winery—Mayacamas, for example—to order as few barrels as it needed and still have them made to order. Barrels are shipped transatlantic in containers that hold 132 to 150, depending on the size of the barrel, and not all wineries could afford or needed that many. When I sold enough to fill a container, we shipped it. I would make out the bill of lading to the winery that bought the largest number of barrels in the container. How did the barrels get distributed? The other buyers picked up their barrels from the one with the bill of lading, and they all apportioned the shipping charges. The system has changed now, but that's how I really got the business going."

While her barrel brokerage expanded, Becky was also helping Philip Diamond set up his wine importing business. He began Diamond Wine Merchants in 1977, and in the beginning he specialized in Burgundies from small estates that Becky chose for him.

In the first years, one of Philip Diamond's best customers for the wines he imported from Becky Wasserman was Mel Knox, who bought them for the San Francisco shop where he was wine buyer. Mel and Becky became good friends, which is why, when she came down with flu on one of her barrel-selling trips to California, she called Mel. "What am I going to do? I've got to get to the wineries, but I can't even get out of bed. What's going to happen?"

"Don't worry," Mel assured her. "Give me your list and let me see what I can do." As a wine buyer, Mel knew most of the winemakers on Becky's list. Without visiting one of them, he was able to get 450 telephone orders for barrels.

Becky was impressed. "If you can do that," she told him, "why don't you take over?"

Mel did. In little more than a year, in fact, he sold so many barrels that Becky asked him to become a full partner in her barrel business. That was in September 1980. A few months later, Mel left the wine shop; since then, he has been a full-time barrel broker.

"When I began with the business," Mel said, "François Frères was making probably about 4,000 barrels a year. It's now making 7,500 barrels. I'm selling to 120 wineries in California, Oregon, Washington and Virginia. I think it's fair to say Becky and I put Jean François on the international market. And yes"—he laughed—"I go to the wineries now. You don't do this much business just by telephone. I also go to France once a year."

Today, Mel Knox works by a different method than the one Becky used. François Frères has set up a corporation in its name in California, and Mel sells part of Jean François's barrels through the corporation. The bill of lading is made out to the *tonnellerie*'s American company or to Mel Knox. A winery can buy any number of barrels from the ones Mel now has in stock in this country, or it can special-order barrels from France and pay for them in either dollars or francs.

About the time that Mel and Becky began to work together, they added another *tonnellerie* to their business. Taransaud has been making barrels in the Cognac region in western France since the 1850s; in 1974, the *tonnellerie* was acquired by Moët-Hennessy, the holding company, formed in 1971, that owns Moët & Chandon Champagne and Hennessy Cognac, among other firms. Becky and Mel became Taransaud's representatives in the United States.

Most of Taransaud's production is in the *barrique,* or Bordeaux barrel, although it fills orders for other sizes and shapes. While François Frères will toast the inside of barrels either medium or heavy, Taransaud obliges its clients with light, medium or heavy toast. It is a *tonnellerie* with a reputation for producing high-quality barrels, and Mel Knox now sells 1,700 to 1,800 of those barrels annually in the United States.

With Mel in charge of the barrel brokerage, Becky was able to pursue her wine brokerage. Earlier, she had taken steps to formalize the business. As a foreigner in France, she needed, first, a *carte de séjour,* or residence card, which she had had since coming to France. Next, she applied for a *carte de commerçant étranger,* which is an authorization allowing a foreigner to establish a company in France.

"It takes about six months to get a *carte de commerçant étranger,*" Becky said. "I had to decide, too, what form the business would take. I opted for a corporation, because I felt that would make it easier in my dealings with banks.

"All this, by the way, is handled by a *notaire.* He's licensed by the government and it is he, not a lawyer, whom you go to see when you want to set up a new business. He's also the person you would see when you're buying or selling property."

The *carte de commerçant étranger* arrived, and as of May 18, 1979, Le Serbet was officially born, a corporation that included a wine brokerage and a barrel brokerage.

As a wine broker, Becky does not own vineyards or a winery or stocks of wine. Instead, she acts as a matchmaker, seeking out wines she likes and then finding a client who likes them too.

When Becky began her wine business, there were other brokers in Burgundy. But she was the only American. She was a woman. She was dealing with the small grower-producer who aged and bottled his own wine. She was, in many ways, an anomaly.

7

MONKS AND MONASTERIES

For all the legends and theories and studies that have been amassed over the years, no one is yet sure who first introduced wine into the region we know as Burgundy. Was it the Phoenicians, coming up from the south centuries before Christ, who offered wine to local Celtic tribes in return for safe passage through the region? And who were the first people to plant and cultivate the grapevine in the thirty-mile ribbon we call the Côte d'Or, the slope of gold?

By the first century B.C., the Romans were writing about vines planted in Gaul, but they made no specific reference to Burgundy. Documents from the early fourth century A.D., however, mention vineyards near Beaune and other Burgundian villages, and describe them as sizable and well established.

But the modern history of Burgundy was really determined two centuries later, in the 580s, when Gontran, King of Burgundy, donated part of his vineyard land to the Abbey of Saint Bénigne.

Early in the next century, Amalgaire, a duke of Burgundy, established the Abbey of Bèze and endowed it with vineyards. In the late 700s, Charlemagne gave vineyards to the Abbey of Saulieu. As Burgundy evolved from a kingdom to a duchy, many other nobles followed the example Gontran had set and donated vineyards to religious orders. The land they gave was in Meursault, Pommard, Chassagne, Gevrey, Vosne, Auxey and other villages. Some centuries later, when they had been properly developed, many of these vineyards represented the best wine land in Burgundy. And much of it belonged to the Church.

Wine, however, represented only one of the luxuries that the more prosperous monasteries enjoyed. Their enormous wealth came from the immense properties they owned, which, in turn, gave them immense power. And none more so than Cluny. A Benedictine monastery founded in 910 in the Mâconnais, Cluny developed many of the vineyards in that southern part of Burgundy from land donated to it. Cluny grew rapidly and soon became the wealthiest and most powerful abbey in the western world.

By the beginning of the twelfth century, it controlled over twelve hundred monasteries and ten thousand monks in France, Germany, Spain, Italy, England, Scotland, Poland and Portugal. Cluny was the leading center of religious influence, and to celebrate its strength, it built Saint Peter and Saint Paul, a Romanesque church that, until Saint Peter's Basilica was erected in Rome, was the largest ecclesiastical building in Europe.

With power and wealth came worldliness, a style of living and of eating and drinking that was far removed from the strict and simple monastic life laid down by Saint Benedict in the sixth century. In his famous Rule, Saint Benedict called for each monk to spend his waking hours divided almost equally into manual work, common prayer and religious reading, contemplation and study. The Rule, only seventy-three short chapters, covered not only every aspect of the formation and administration of a Benedictine monastery, the training of novices, the prayers of the Opus Dei, or Divine Office, and even how much wine a monk was allowed to drink, but it also outlined, in chapters 5, 6 and 7, the principal monastic virtues—obedience, silence and humility.

Throughout France, there were Benedictines who looked at the wealthier abbeys, particularly at Cluny, and felt their monks had forgotten about humility and obedience and manual labor.

One of them was Robert, abbot of Molesmes, a monastery north of Dijon between Laignes and les Riceys, which was founded in 1075. Robert had tried to enact reform at Molesmes, but he was not satisfied with the results; in 1098, he left the abbey with twenty companions who shared his desire to return to the strict observance of the Rule of Saint Benedict.

On the flat plains of Burgundy's eastern edge, on a stretch of marshes scattered with swamps and reeds in a clearing within forests of oaks—land donated by his cousin Raynard, Viscount of Beaune—Robert established a new monastery. His purpose was to create a reformed commune, not to start a new order, and for some years the establishment was known simply as the New Monastery. The Old French word for the reed that surrounded the monastery was *cistel.* From *cistel,* the name evolved to the Latin Cistercium and Cistellium. In 1120, when the monastery had already become the center of the new Cistercian order, it was renamed Cîteaux.

In 1099, the ecclesiastical powers forced Robert to return to Molesmes. Alberic succeeded him at the New Monastery, and after his death, Stephen Harding, an Englishman, became its head. It was under one of these two strong abbots that Cîteaux showed its singular nature by rejecting all feudal revenues, basing its economy instead solely on the manual labor of the monks. Despite strong leadership and hard work by the monks, however, Cîteaux remained a small monastery, suffering in its early years from extreme poverty and few recruits.

All this was to change, through two very different forces.

One was the arrival in 1112 of the young Bernard de Fontaine (later Saint Bernard), with thirty companions. One year later, he took his vows. A man with a magnetic personality, Bernard violently denounced the luxurious life of some of his Benedictine brothers and vented most of his anger against those of Cluny.

As monks began to leave Cîteaux to establish daughter houses, or new monasteries, Cîteaux became the seat of the new Cistercian order. La Ferté was established as early as 1113; Pontigny, in 1114. Three years after his arrival, Bernard left Cîteaux to establish another daughter house, the Abbey of Clairvaux. He became its abbot and set about practicing a life of severe austerity, creating a prime example for the new order.

As Bernard's fame grew, so did the order, spreading rapidly through France, Italy, Germany, England, Austria and Spain by 1132. At the time of Bernard's death, in 1153, the Cistercians had three hundred daughter houses, sixty-five of which Bernard had personally established. By the beginning of the next century, the Cistercians had over five hundred, and Cîteaux itself had evolved from a small, impoverished monastery into one of the richest and most powerful abbeys in Europe.

Another aspect of Cîteaux's historical importance also began in the early twelfth century. Soon after Robert had founded the monastery, it became apparent that the surrounding marshland would never yield grapes, no matter how much the monks worked and prayed. Unable to grow vines on their own land, a small group of monks followed the narrow Vouge River until, about a dozen miles northwest of Cîteaux, they found uncultivated fields on a gentle slope that was warmed by sunshine and seemed right to them for grapevines. The monks bartered with four Burgundian landowners, exchanging a small sum of money, two cotton tunics and a promise of eternal salvation for seven acres of the slope.

And that was how Clos de Vougeot was born. Other Burgundian noblemen heard about the priceless promise of eternal salvation, and soon they, too, were donating land and vineyards to Cîteaux. By the fourteenth century, and possibly earlier, Vougeot had grown to about its present size of 125 acres, the largest single vineyard in Burgundy. It was named Vougeot after the streamlike Vouge River, and Cîteaux owned all of it, as well as other valuable vineyards stretching from Dijon south to Meursault.

At Vougeot, the monks of Cîteaux cleared their first seven acres and planted vines. Then they built the *cellier,* a storage cellar with eight huge stone pillars to support the fifty-foot oak beams of the ceiling, and with lancet windows for light. Next they built the *cuverie*—the press and fermenting room—and four gigantic winepresses made of oak from the forests of Cîteaux. Above the *cellier* there was an attic that served as a dormitory for the monks and lay brothers who came from Cîteaux to work at Vougeot.

And work they did. It was the medieval monks, especially the Cistercians with their dedication to manual labor, who formed the great vineyards and the great wines of Burgundy. Unlike laic vineyard owners, the monks were not pressed to earn a profit each year. They spent years studying a problem in the vine or wines. They worked at improving their methods of pruning and cultivation. If the vines died of disease, as they often did, they began again. They planted and replanted and studied the results. They were the first to notice that there were subtle differences between vineyards and even parts of the same vineyard, and that these fine distinctions produced wines that differed from each other often by the most delicate shadings. They had the invaluable asset that few others had—or have. Time.

Vougeot was walled, probably in the thirteenth or fourteenth century, soon after it had reached its present size, and thus became a *clos,* or walled enclosure.

In the sixteenth century, Dom Jean Loisier, the forty-eighth abbot of Cîteaux, added a château to Vougeot's winery buildings —Renaissance elegance wedded to medieval monastic practicality in the midst of a sea of vineyards. For the next two centuries, the monks at Clos de Vougeot went about their work, refining their grape-growing and winemaking techniques, studying and recording their findings and producing wondrous wines. The Cistercians were the great vineyardists of their time.

Then, in 1789, the French Revolution began. By 1791, the new government dissolved all Cistercian monasteries. The Abbey of Cîteaux, its daughter houses and its annexes including Clos de Vougeot were confiscated and declared the property of the state. The abbey was sold, and the twelfth-century buildings were destroyed.

During the 1800s, Cîteaux, its vineyards ripped from it, was for a time a sugar factory and then, for ten years, a cooperative community of people who followed the philosophy of François Charles Marie Fourier, a sociologist and reformer. In 1864, the former abbey was bought by Père Joseph Rey, who made it a colony for troubled and delinquent children.

It was these adolescent boys who, with Père Rey, rebuilt the church that had been destroyed after the revolution.

The number of children under Père Rey's care increased rapidly, so that by the time of his death, in 1873, there were 830 living at the colony.

After Père Rey's death, Monseigneur Oury, bishop of Dijon, was concerned that Cîteaux might pass into the hands of the state, and in 1895 he proposed to the Cistercian order that it buy back Cîteaux. With the financial help of Baroness de La Rochetaillée, the domaine was purchased; the monastery that had given birth to the Cistercians once again belonged to the Cistercians.

In 1898, eight hundred years after Robert of Molesmes founded it, Cîteaux reopened as an abbey.

8

CÎTEAUX

The young Cistercian monks looked up, startled to see a woman in their small dairy. Except in church, where worshipers from the "outside" occasionally come, the monks have few visitors at the Abbey of Cîteaux. Within the abbey walls, visitors are even scarcer, and women are virtually never seen. But one of the rules the Cistercians live by is "You will love silence," and so the monks stole a few quick glances at me, remained silent and continued their work.

I had arrived at Cîteaux early one morning in the fall of 1984 for an appointment that had taken months, and the intervention of a good friend of the abbey, to obtain. In the cool, dark reception room, I met Frère Frédéric, the monk who was to take me behind the wall of Cîteaux. We walked down a long corridor and took a right down another corridor. At the end of it, he opened a door. As I walked through, I stepped into another world, one that juxtaposed the eighteenth century, the Middle Ages, a whisper of times earlier still and a mouse squeak's worth of today.

When Cîteaux reopened more than a century after it was closed by the French Revolution, the monks had to find means of supporting the abbey and themselves. Cheese became their main source of income.

"The monks may very well have made some cheese before the revolution," said Frère Frédéric, who is in charge of the abbey's financial affairs, "but it only became a major economic factor after we reopened. Up to World War I, Cîteaux produced a firmer cheese, similar to Gruyère. Now, as you see, we make this disk-shaped cheese that is buttery." Most of them weigh 750 grams (about 1⅔ pounds), but they vary by about 100 grams one way or another.

In the dairy, the monks went about their work quietly, making cheeses whose exterior will mature to a pale salmon-tinged yellow imprinted with the weave of the cloth wrapped around them during pressing. Inside will be a delicious smooth yellow paste with small, irregular holes, a mildly tangy taste that finishes with a light bite.

"We make about 230 cheeses a day," Frère Frédéric explained. "Our milk comes from eighty cows of the Montbéliarde species, which is part of the Pirouge breed. It takes seven liters of milk to make one kilo of cheese most of the year, almost eight liters in summer, when the cows drink more water."

We watched as the monks poured the fresh milk into a stainless-steel vat and heated it to 95 degrees Fahrenheit. (The milk is not pasteurized.) Rennet, a natural coagulant that comes from the stomach of a calf, was added, and within a half hour the milk had separated into curd (white lumps resembling soft custard) and whey (a thin, sweet, cloudy liquid). After the whey had been drained off, the curd mass was formed into disks, which the monks put into cloth-lined circular molds and placed under a press for five minutes. They then removed the cheese, flipped it over, rewrapped it loosely in the cloth, put it back in the mold and placed it under the press, where it stays for twenty-four hours. The next day, the cheeses will be salted and taken to the cellars, where they are aged for three to four weeks before going to market.

About two thirds of the cheeses are sold in a small shop, operated by two elderly monks, in the outer wall of the abbey. Aside from the church, it is the only part of the abbey that is open to the public. The rest of the cheeses are sold in Dijon (fourteen miles to the north) and in Beaune (ten miles to the south). The cheese, which, like the abbey, is called Cîteaux, accounts for half of the abbey's income.

Cîteaux is settled on nearly six hundred acres about eight and a half miles east of the small town of Nuits-Saint-Georges. The monks rent out about one hundred acres, and they work the remaining acres themselves. They grow wheat and barley, and corn and other grains for animal feed; and they raise cattle and a few pigs, which they sell for butchering.

There is little standing of the old Cîteaux—the façade of a fifteenth-century library, arcades of a Gothic cloister, a commendable eighteenth-century building. What does remain is an aura of timelessness. As Frère Frédéric and I walked across the farm, a monk passed. With the hood of his robe pulled up over his head, he was a medieval silhouette, albeit one in *bleu de travaille,* the bright blue of workmen's clothes in France, rather than the Cistercians' traditional brown or white. To one side, another monk tended a few of the abbey's white-and-maroon-shaded cows. From the dairy, a monk appeared pushing a wheelbarrow loaded with cheeses. With seemingly no thought of the Burgundy that lay less than ten miles to the west, they moved about silently, purposefully, as though by their work they were polishing their souls. But just as the world began to feel centuries younger, just as a feather-light mantle of peace enveloped me, there was a faint, persistent, very contemporary sound. Frère Frédéric reached into his leather-belted brown robe and shut off his beeper.

"Excuse me; I have a telephone call."

While I waited for him, I looked across fields where Saint Bernard may have walked nearly nine hundred years ago. There was a monochromatic stillness about the farm; through it, I heard the recurring echo of a beep.

Frère Frédéric, a tall, slim, ascetic-looking man with close-cropped graying hair, studied geophysics before entering Cîteaux twenty-six years ago. "We spend five years here before taking vows. We have time to think about our choice. Those five years are spent within the abbey," he said, "away from the temptations of the world outside Cîteaux, which may help make the choice easier and the decision more lasting." Most of the men enter the monastery when they are in their early twenties, and according to Frère Frédéric, it is rare to have one leave after he has taken vows. "In my years at Cîteaux, I remember only one monk who left."

Because of the nature of his work, Frère Frédéric is one of the few monks at Cîteaux who has regular contact with the outside world. For most of Cîteaux's fifty monks, life is restricted

Frère Frédéric at the Abbey of Cîteaux.

and reclusive, and while they are told to love rather than to practice silence, theirs is a quiet world that revolves around prayer, meditation and manual labor. In chapters 48 and 57 of his Rule, Saint Benedict describes this labor as agricultural, domestic or artisan in nature. At Cîteaux, the monks work in the fields, with the cows or in the dairy. Some learn to be mechanics. Some learn to cook. In summer, one of the monks bakes bread. In winter, the abbey buys bread because the breadmaking monk is also in charge of central heating, a system that is fed manually with wood and allows little time for baking bread.

Whatever kind of work he performs, every monk at Cîteaux does something that contributes to the abbey and his own upkeep. Even monasteries devoted to medieval thoughts are aware that the price of keeping oneself in bed, board and hooded robes rises. "In 1981, it cost forty-five francs a day to support a monk," Frère Frédéric said. "Today, it costs seventy francs a day. That includes food, clothing, heat, the upkeep of the building. Everything."

The rigorous, ordered life that Saint Bernard prescribed and lived himself remains the foundation of the monks' day. And they adhere as strictly to the sixth-century Rule of Saint Benedict as the late twentieth century will allow.

Divided into canonical hours on which the Divine Office of the order is based, the Cistercian day begins at 3:45 A.M., when the monks rise. By 4 A.M., they are in church for the night office, which lasts an hour. At 5 A.M., they begin an hour of private meditation; then, after a simple breakfast, they return to church at 6:45 A.M. for the office of lauds, followed by mass.

At 8 A.M., they meet with the abbey's superior for fifteen minutes and then go to La Salle du Chapitre, a room where, each morning, one chapter—which is one page—of the Rule of Saint Benedict is read aloud. From there, they spend thirty minutes in religious contemplation and then return to church for tierce, a fifteen-minute office. For those whose workday has already begun—the monks milking cows or Frère Frédéric, who may have to be in his office, for example—the prayer is said silently, by themselves. After tierce, everyone works until noon, when they gather in church again, for the office of sexte, followed by a lunch of fish, vegetables and salad (the Cistercians eat no meat).

A monk at the Abbey of Cîteaux with a wheelbarrow of cheeses.

At 1:15 P.M., they have leisure time when they might read or listen to music or take a walk. At 2 P.M., they go to church for the office of nones, and then they return to work.

At 5 P.M., there is another hour devoted to religious thought. At 6 P.M. they meet in church for vespers, followed by fifteen minutes of meditation. Dinner is a simple, self-service affair of soup and vegetables, cheese, fruit and bread. At 7 P.M., they gather for a short meeting and then return to church for compline, the last office of the day, finishing with "Salve Regina," which is the only song the Cistercians still sing in Latin. And they go to bed, to rise again at 3:45 A.M.

The hours may change slightly, beginning perhaps fifteen minutes earlier or later, depending on the season. But the schedule never varies.

The oldest monk living at Cîteaux is eighty-eight-year-old Frère Guy, who for forty years made the abbey's cheese. One day, Frère Frédéric asked Frère Guy if, in his long life at the abbey, he had ever been sad or lonely or felt a twinge of regret.

"How could I?" Frère Guy answered. "I never had time."

About seventy miles south of Cîteaux, where Cluny once reigned as the richest and most influential abbey of Europe, there is now mostly ruin. Cluny was closed in 1790. Two years later, the town council issued an order to demolish the buildings and sell the stones. By 1825, Cluny had been nearly totally destroyed.

Of the largest ecclesiastical building in the medieval world, the Church of Saint Peter and Saint Paul, there remain little more than the south transept, a fifteenth-century chapel, a tower and a belfry.

In the thirteenth-century building where flour was kept, there is a small museum of stone carvings and capitals and other ruins. There are some towers. And one large, imposing building, restored and transformed in 1873, has remarkable cloisters and staircases and a grand façade that look onto a garden. It now houses the École Nationale Superieure d'Arts et Métiers, usually referred to by its students as ENSAM. Other than the school, there is a reception room where the visitor buys a ticket and waits for a guided tour through the ruins. Of all the grandeur that was Cluny, this is all that is left.

After Clos de Vougeot was taken from Cîteaux, it changed hands often, and only occasionally did all the vineyards belong to one person or family. The last time, in fact, that they were under one ownership was in the nineteenth century. Since then, the domaine's 125 acres have been bought in small plots, so that currently over seventy *vignerons* own portions of the vineyard. Meanwhile, without the Cistercians to care for it, the château began to deteriorate. In 1889, a Burgundian named Léonce Bocquet bought it and spent great sums of money to restore it.

In 1944, the château of Clos de Vougeot was purchased by the Confrérie des Chevaliers du Tastevin, an international wine society whose purpose is to spread the good word about Burgundy's wines while its members eat, drink and make merry, an exercise they do often at the château, at spectacular dinners held in the great stone-and-oak *cellier*.

Of all their dinners, perhaps the most glorious is the one held during Les Trois Glorieuses, Burgundy's annual three-day celebration surrounding the wine auction of the Hospices de Beaune. On the third weekend of November, the medieval town of Beaune, which lives on wine and stands on millions of gallons of wine in its labyrinthine cellars, is the center of the festivities.

The weekend is a dizzy whirl that turns from tasting to luncheon to tasting to dinner. On Sunday afternoon, the auction takes place. The Hospices was founded in 1443 as a charitable hospital by Nicolas Rolin, chancellor to the Duke of Burgundy, and his wife, Guigone de Salins. Today, it is Beaune's major tourist attraction, a stunning example of Burgundian and Flemish architecture whose stone façade is topped with a steeply sloping roof tiled in diamond-shaped patterns of red, white, yellow and black. Almost from the inception of the Hospices, it became the custom for Burgundians to donate parcels of vineyards to it. Since 1851, these wines have been sold at the annual November auction, providing funds to operate the Hospices.

Les Trois Glorieuses refers to the three glorious events that surround the auction: dinner at Clos de Vougeot on Saturday evening; dinner at the Hospices, which is also known as the Hôtel Dieu, on Sunday evening; and a wonderful, boisterous luncheon, called *La Paulée,* held in the village of Meursault on Monday.

In 1981, as we drove up to Clos de Vougeot for its annual November celebration, the moon was full and the stars were bright, and the château, ablaze with light, seemed to float above its vineyards. In the old *cellier* were five hundred people, dazzling in their gowns and jewels and formal wear, and many of the confrères in red velvet robes and hats. We feasted on foie gras, a cassoulet of seafood, wild boar, cheese, petits fours and more wines than any of us could remember. The actor Peter Ustinov was that year's host, leading the revelers through Burgundian jokes and drinking songs. We sang. We clapped. We laughed and cheered. It was an evening of rollicking, spirited joy and wild, noisy pleasures that resounded throughout the huge wine cellar, against its stone pillars, its oak beams and its lancet windows, built by the Cistercians so many centuries before.

At Cîteaux, the monks no longer drink the wines of Clos de Vougeot. When they take wine with their meals now, it is wine that they buy or that has been given to the abbey. There is one bottle on the table for every four monks, and while the Rule of Saint Benedict speaks of one *émine* of wine per monk, which is about a third of a liter, some drink their share, others drink very little.

That they no longer drink wine they make seems not to matter. What does matter is that it was their brothers, earlier Cistercians, who did more to create the great wines of Burgundy than any other group of people. What matters is that they transformed 125 acres of pastureland into one of France's most famous and enduring vineyards. What also matters is that while the great Cluny is a silent mausoleum and hundreds of other medieval monasteries are no more than rubble, Cîteaux lives.

9

FROM REVOLUTION TO THE EVE

OF EVOLUTION

If Burgundy's great vineyards were born with the Cistercians, their patchwork pattern was born with the French Revolution. When the uprising struck, many of Burgundy's most prized vineyards were owned by the Cistercians and other religious orders. In the aftermath of the revolution, all these vineyards, as well as some of the vineyards belonging to the nobility, were seized by the state, often split into small parcels and sold to the people of Burgundy. Over the years, many of those noblemen who had managed to retain their vineyards during the upheaval sold them, usually in sections, to the region's bourgeoisie.

The new owners in turn often split them further when they left the vineyards to their children, dividing the land equally among them. The size and shape of the vineyards were rarely affected by this partitioning; in fact, nearly all the major vineyards have remained entities, with their boundaries pretty much as they were before the revolution. But within those boundaries, multiple inheritances spread over the generations have often divided a vineyard among several owners.

In vineyards that are divided, each owner may hold a fraction of the whole; yet he works his fraction apart from the rest as if it were a vineyard unto itself. In this way, the revolution did not much change the face of Burgundy, but it changed forever its form and character.

One result of this multi-ownership of a vineyard is that two wines produced by different vintners from grapes grown in the same vineyard can taste somewhat different from each other.

The differences may be caused by the age of the vines, with older vines giving more concentrated and deeper flavors; by the care taken of that part of the vineyard; or by the skills of the winemaker. The differences could also be the effect of the size or location of the vintner's property. As the Cistercians discovered, vineyards lying no more than a path apart from each other, and even different parts of one large vineyard, can, because of variations in soil and exposure to the sun, yield grapes that differ slightly. If a vintner has only a small segment of a vineyard and harvests perhaps only a thousand pounds of grapes, he may have too little to blend into a wine that is representative of that vineyard appellation as a whole.

Because ownership of a small part of one vineyard is not enough to provide a living and support a family, vintners usually have small holdings in a number of vineyards. Thus, a grower might own a section of the village appellation Gevrey-Chambertin; some *ouvrées* (an *ouvrée* is just over a tenth of an acre) of a First Growth vineyard within Gevrey-Chambertin; perhaps a few *ouvrées* in Vosne-Romanée or Chambolle-Musigny; and a larger piece of a regional appellation like Bourgogne rouge. In this way, he could hold perhaps ten or fifteen acres, yet he would have only a small part of any one important vineyard.

Under this pattern of ownership, many vintners soon felt that the wine they made from a single parcel of vineyard did not warrant their aging, bottling and marketing the wine under their own labels. From this situation, the *négociant* system emerged. For the most part, the *négociant* buys young wine from the small producers, blends wines that are from the same appellation and ages the blend. In some cases, when a *négociant* can buy a quantity of exceptionally good wine, he will not blend it, but instead will keep it separate to preserve its singular personality. In other cases, a *négociant* will also have his own vineyards, whose wines he keeps separate. Louis Latour, for example, owns over one hundred acres, including excellent parcels in Corton and Corton-Charlemagne, and they constitute some of the best wines produced by the Latour establishment.

In a particularly interesting arrangement, Marquis de Laguiche, owner of nearly four and a half acres of Montrachet (the largest single holding of this exalted vineyard) as well as a slice of a Chassagne-Montrachet First Growth, has turned over complete control of them to the *négociant* firm Joseph Drouhin. The firm's current head, Robert Drouhin, is therefore in charge of the marquis's vineyards as well as the making, aging and marketing of the wine.

Still, no matter what the origin of the wine—a blend, a single lot of wine finished by the *négociant*—the label bears the *négociant*'s name. Even the white-and-gold label of the marquis's wine, which reads "Montrachet, Marquis de Laguiche," has the name of Joseph Drouhin above and below.

From the nineteenth century until after World War II, this is the way most of the wines of Burgundy were marketed.

While political change refashioned Burgundy's character, two major physical disasters during the nineteenth century altered the way most of Europe's vineyards were to be planted and grown and treated. The first of these disasters, oïdium, or powdery mildew, hit in the mid-1850s and threatened Burgundy as it did vineyards throughout the Continent. A disease that attacks the leaves and splits the berries, it will kill an untreated vine within a few years. Fortunately, a treatment—finely powdered sulfur—was found that would keep the disease at bay. To be effective, however, the treatment had to be used many times during each growing season. Today, thousands of tons of a mixture of sulfur and copper are still sprayed on the grapevines of France alone each year to protect them against oïdium.

No sooner was oïdium under control than phylloxera, a far more destructive disease, struck in the 1860s. It was brought to England unknowingly on native American vines of the *Vitis labrusca* species, which were themselves immune to it. A burrowing plant louse, phylloxera kills by attacking the roots of a vine. From England, phylloxera spread to the Continent, hopping from one region to the next and devastating nearly all the vineyards of the winemaking countries. It arrived in the Côte d'Or in the late 1870s.

For more than a generation, no one knew how to stop it. Dozens of possible solutions were suggested, but only two methods gave promising, albeit conditional, results. One method was flooding the vineyards, which did indeed kill the louse, but it was a solution applicable only to flat sites. The other method was pumping carbon bisulfide into the soil where the louse lived, a dangerous operation, for the chemical was toxic as well as easily inflammable and explosive. It, too, killed the louse, but it did not protect the vineyard from reinfection. Although both methods worked in their circumscribed ways, neither provided a universal answer.

The answer came when the French accepted the fact that they had to graft their European vines, which belong to the *Vitis vinifera* species, to the phylloxera-immune rootstocks of native American grapevine species. Thus, the vines that had brought the problem ultimately stemmed the problem, and today most of the *Vitis vinifera* vines in the western world are planted on rootstock of the American species.

The French have passed wine laws for centuries. Some laws limited the area in which certain wines could be made. Others named wines and protected those names, or demanded that only certain grape varieties could be grown. The earliest of these laws probably dates back to the late fourteenth century, when Philip the Bold, Duke of Burgundy, banned the Gamay grape from Burgundy, stating that the "Gaamez made a wine of a . . . horrible harshness." In the next century, Charles VI enacted a law that said the wines of a given region, which included wines made in the Auxerrois and the Beaunois and that traveled on the Yonne River, should be called Vins de Bourgogne.

Through the next four centuries, many more wine decrees were passed regionally. But nothing that could be considered national or major wine legislation was enacted until the beginning of the twentieth century. The first of these, the 1905 Act, limited some of the abuses that came about when the death and slow rebirth of the vineyards after their destruction by phylloxera caused acute shortages of wine. For the most part, the 1905 Act protected the wine consumer by making the vintner declare the amount of wine he had made in a year and by allowing a wine to carry a place of origin on its label only if it came from the area where wines of that type were produced. In other words, a

[56]

vigneron on the Côte de Provence could not legally label his wine "Bourgogne." Still, the law was only a beginning, raising more questions than it answered. A series of interim laws were passed over the three decades after its passage, fine-tuning geographic delimitations, grape varieties and many other points regarding soil, production and vinification.

Then, in 1935, France enacted the world's first comprehensive wine legislation, known as the Appellation d'Origine Contrôlée (A.O.C.), or "controlled place of origin," laws, which cover all aspects of winemaking, from soil and varietal to label.

To begin with, it limits the place of origin of a wine. Because the French believe soil gives wine its basic characteristics and climate affects its quality, the geographic location of a vineyard is of prime importance. As a result, only those vineyards located within the defined boundaries of a given area and capable of producing wines that are typical of that area have the right to use its appellation.

It also specifies the grape varietals that can be grown in an appellation area, based on *"les usages locaux, loyaux et constants,"* the local, loyal and constant customs that are really the key to the entire structure of the A.O.C. laws. These customs, in turn, are based on centuries of proof that there is a reciprocal exchange between grape and soil. Built on the foundation of these local customs, the A.O.C. laws allow only those varieties that have proved best for a region's soil to be planted in that region's vineyards.

A.O.C. controls the minimum alcohol content for each wine. The maximum yield of grapes per acre is also specified, the theory being that if more grapes are produced per acre, they tend to have less concentration of flavor. Yet this yield can be legally adjusted—increased or decreased—if the year is exceptional enough to warrant it.

Also specified by law is the winemaking procedures that have, through tradition, become part of a region's practices.

The A.O.C. laws, formed to a great extent by the growers of each region and based on each region's wine tradition, are regulated and supervised by the I.N.A.O.—Institut National des Appellations d'Origine (National Institute of Place Names)—in Paris.

I.N.A.O. also controls chaptalization, the practice of adding sugar to the must (the fermenting grape juice) in most years, to complete the structure of the wine when there is not enough natural sugar in the grape. Because it is sugar that ferments into approximately half alcohol and half carbon dioxide, which escapes, grapes with too little sugar cannot produce a wine with adequate alcohol. If the alcohol content is too low, a wine will have little staying power and will taste out of balance. I.N.A.O. allows only some wine regions to chaptalize, and in those regions, it sets the amount of chaptalization that may be used. The practice of adding sugar to must dates back at least two hundred years, when the Cistercians reportedly used sugar to help their wines in poor years.

Chaptalization is used in many of the world's cooler wine regions—throughout Germany, and in the French regions of Burgundy, Alsace and Champagne, for example. It is also used in some years in Bordeaux.

It is a legal and often a necessary step to make a sound wine. Problems arise not in the use but in the abuse of the method. If a grower allows his vineyards to overproduce and then relies on chaptalization to mask inadequacies in that wine, that is abuse. If so much sugar is added that the wine tastes anonymous, that is abuse.

"When wines are overchaptalized," Becky Wasserman says, "they tend to lose the character of their particular appellation, the special character that comes from the *terroir,* the soil."

"When chaptalization is done correctly," adds Lalou Bize-Leroy, director of Maison Leroy, *négociants,* and co-director of Domaine de la Romanée-Conti, "it can help give a wine a little more structure. On average, adding only enough sugar to raise the alcohol by one degree is correct."

The region defined as Viticultural Burgundy, producing A.O.C., or controlled-appellation, wines, spreads over four departments. In the north, separated from the Côte d'Or by some seventy miles, is Chablis, in the department of the Yonne. South of the Côte d'Or, in the department of Saône-et-Loire, there are, first, the Côte Chalonnaise and, below it, the Mâconnais. Still farther south, in the department of the Rhône, is Beaujolais.

The heart of Burgundy—both geographically and spiritually—is the Côte d'Or, where a glorious ribbon of vineyards runs along the thirty-mile stretch of western hills. Many of the hillsides are topped with close clusters of trees that stand like tall bristled brushes, while the vineyards, all of which face east and southeast, reach sensuously toward the sun on its long arc across the sky to dusk.

The northern part of the Côte d'Or, called the Côte de Nuits, begins below Dijon with the village of Fixin and, going south, follows through such famed wine villages as Gevrey-Chambertin, Morey-Saint-Denis, Chambolle-Musigny, Vougeot, Vosne-Romanée and Nuits-Saint-Georges. Most of the wines of the Côte de Nuits are red.

The southern part of the Côte d'Or is named the Côte de Beaune, after the medieval town that is the wine center of Burgundy.

Starting a few miles south of Nuits-Saint-Georges is a string of Côte de Beaune wine villages, including Ladoix, Pernand-Verglesses, Aloxe-Corton, Savigny-lès-Beaune, Beaune, Pommard, Volnay, Monthélie, Meursault, Auxey-Duresses, Saint-Romain, Puligny-Montrachet, Chassagne-Montrachet and Santennay. While the Côte de Beaune produces both red and white wine and has garnered fame for both, it is noted mostly for its whites, even though they account for only 27.6 percent of its A.O.C. production.

In Burgundy, all of the great white wines are made from the noble Chardonnay grape. The great reds of the Côte d'Or and the reds of the Chalonnais are produced from the equally noble Pinot Noir, while the reds of the Mâconnais and Beaujolais are made from the Gamay grape. Other white wines of Burgundy are made from Aligoté.

All are grapes that have grown in Burgundy for centuries. Burgundy also has a regional blend called Passetoutgrains—by law, two-thirds Gamay and one-third Pinot Noir, although some vintners use more Pinot and less Gamay.

As in all of France's wine regions, Burgundy's vineyard names are controlled by the A.O.C. laws. Burgundy, however, with its myriad small patches sliced from each other like parts of an intricate jigsaw puzzle and differing from each other often by the slightest variation of style in its wines, creates a complex picture. In the thirty miles of the Côte d'Or, there are some five dozen appellations; they are classified into four major categories.

The broadest is the regional appellation, which encompasses wines whose grapes grow anywhere within the defined region of Burgundy. The five regional appellations are Bourgogne, Bourgogne Grand Ordinaire, Bourgogne Passetoutgrains, Bourgogne Aligoté, and Crémant de Bourgogne (a lightly sparkling wine).

From this broad appellation, Burgundy moves to village appellations. These are wines made from grapes grown in the designated vineyards of a particular village, or commune, such as Volnay, Pommard or Vosne-Romanée. In total, there are twenty-five village appellations in the Côte d'Or. A label on a village appellation wine would read, for example, "Appellation Volnay Contrôlée."

Moving up the scale of quality are individually named vineyards within a village that are considered superior because of their particular soil and location. The first step above the village appellation are the *Premier Cru,* or First Growth, vineyards. The wines of these vineyards are labeled, first, with the village name, then with either the vineyard name or the phrase *Premier Cru,* or both. Take, for instance, the *Premier Cru* vineyard Grèves in Beaune. Its label can read "Beaune-Grèves," "Beaune Premier Cru" or "Beaune-Grèves Premier Cru." Whatever phrase is used, the label will also include the phrase "Appellation Contrôlée." The Côte d'Or has so many *Premier Cru* vineyards that no one has been able to give me a figure. When asked, most Burgundians simply throw up their hands.

The most distinguished wines of Burgundy are those of the *Grand Cru,* or Great Growth, vineyards. Because of their reputation as the finest of Burgundy, these wines can be labeled solely with their vineyard name, such as Montrachet, Corton, Chambertin and La Tâche. The Côte de Nuits has twenty-three *Grands Crus,* the Côte de Beaune has eight *Grands Crus,* and each of these thirty-one special vineyards is an appellation in itself.

In the way of Burgundy, most of the great vineyards, too, are divided into slivers. Montrachet, for instance, is 18½ acres; yet it has thirteen owners. In fact, of the thirty-one *Grands Crus,* only four remain under single owners. They are Romanée-Conti (4½ acres), La Tâche (about 15 acres) and La Romanée (barely 2 acres), all in Vosne-Romanée; and Clos de Tart, an 18¾-acre vineyard in Morey-Saint-Denis.

It should be noted that over the years some villages have hyphenated the name of their most famous *Grand Cru* vineyard to their own name. Thus, for example, Gevrey is now Gevrey-Chambertin, Aloxe is Aloxe-Corton and Chambolle is Chambolle-Musigny.

Given the complicated tangle of Burgundy's vineyards, one can understand how the big *négociants* thrived. For the small grower, selling his young wine to them meant quick payment, with neither the expense or bother of aging and bottling his wines nor the concern of finding importers for his small production. Nor did he have to convince importers that his Volnay or Meursault or Gevrey-Chambertin *Premier Cru* was more evocative of that vineyard than one bottled by a large *négociant*.

For the small grower, however, his wines became nameless. And while not all *négociants* succumbed to the habit of developing a "house style"—which meant that all wines under a given label were recognized by the style of that *négociant* rather than by that of the wine's appellation—those who did highlight their own house style negated the most characteristic facet of Burgundy's wine, the individuality that the soil of each appellation imparts to the wine.

The efforts of the Cistercians to differentiate between *Crus* and the habit of some laic shippers to obliterate these special identities faced each other across a gap of eight hundred years.

10

ESTATE BOTTLING

Quietly and in a small way, an evolution began in Burgundy some fifty years ago. The evolution was a gradual move toward estate bottling, and since its first major stir, it has continued to gather momentum.

To be sure, the strength of the *négociant,* and especially of the honest *négociant* of fine wine, is still clad in iron. But there has been a delicate shift of balance, a subtle dissemination of power, as more vintners age and bottle their own wines. It is as though seeds have germinated in that mystical soil of Burgundy, flowering in a burst of personal pride.

Like all such moves in which hundreds, perhaps thousands, are affected, the core has been the work of the few. A very small number of *vignerons* began bottling part or all of their own wines early, a few in the late nineteenth century, some after World War I, and others just before World War II. Domaine de la Romanée-Conti was bottling part of its Romanée-Conti vineyard by 1929. Soon after, all of Romanée-Conti, part of its Richebourg vineyard and some of the Domaine's other vineyards were also being estate-bottled.

Marquis Jacques d'Angerville of Volnay was also an early proponent of estate bottling. He began after World War I, exporting his wines directly to England and Switzerland; by the 1930s, he was sending them to the United States. Henri Gouges of Nuits-Saint-Georges and Armand Rousseau of Gevrey-Chambertin started bottling some of their wines in the 1920s. André Ramonet of Chassagne-Montrachet was another early estate bottler, and so was Joseph Matrot of Meursault.

They and a few others built the foundation. On it, estate bottling in Burgundy grew slowly, suffering a difficult birth in many cases. Not all vintners made wine worthy of being aged and bottled personally by them. Not all of those who made fine wines understood the intricacies of aging and finishing and bottling or had the equipment to do so. But they learned, often with the encouragement of people from outside the region.

Perhaps the single most influential person in pushing Burgundy toward estate bottling was Raymond Baudouin, a Frenchman from Montargis, a town south of Paris. Monsieur Baudouin had created the magazine *Revue du Vin de France* in 1927. He was also the wine buyer for Taillevent, La Pyramide and other fine restaurants in France. Not long after Monsieur Baudouin started the *Revue,* he met Frank Schoonmaker at Le Roy Gourmet in Paris, one of the restaurants the young American journalist frequented on his many trips to France.

When Frank Schoonmaker left Princeton after only one year, he told his father, a writer and political commentator, that he felt he would learn more by going to Europe. During his hiking and bicycling through the Continent, he visited many wine regions, Burgundy among them. His first articles and books were about his travels. But wine became his great love, and in 1933 his first book on the subject, *Complete Wine Book,* was published. It was during his research for that book that he met Raymond Baudouin. The two became good friends, and under the Frenchman's tutelage, Schoonmaker developed from a knowledgeable, experienced wine amateur into a seasoned, intrepid professional.

Prohibition ended in the United States in December 1933, and soon after, Frank Schoonmaker became a salesman for Bellows & Co., an import firm in New York City that dealt in fine wines. The president of Bellows was Colonel Frederick Wildman. In 1935, Schoonmaker and some friends founded their own wine importing firm, naming it Bates & Schoonmaker. Raymond Baudouin was Schoonmaker's buyer, and beginning that year, the two men made a series of buying trips, searching throughout Burgundy for vintners whose wines they liked and in many cases convincing these vintners to bottle their own wine and sell it to Bates & Schoonmaker. Among the wines they admired were some made by vintners who had already begun estate bottling. One was Marquis d'Angerville. According to his son, also named Jacques, the first wine Schoonmaker imported for his new company in 1935 was probably the late marquis's Volnay Fremiet Premier Cru 1929. The Baudouin-Schoonmaker trips continued until World War II halted them.

Immediately after Pearl Harbor, Frank Schoonmaker was in the OSS, the American intelligence service. He served in Spain and North Africa and took part in the landing at Saint Tropez.

As soon as he was demobilized after the war, Frank Schoonmaker returned to his wine work. As a journalist, he wrote articles. As an author, he wrote books. As an importer, he ferreted out those vintners whose wines he wanted to see bottled under their own labels. He would cajole them, appeal to their pride. "Your wine will be yours. Your name will become famous," he told any vintner who was not sure he wanted the extra burden of estate bottling. In the end, he convinced many of them. In the end, many sent their wines to the United States under their own label and bearing the strip label "Frank Schoonmaker Selections." By then, the import company was Frank Schoonmaker's own.

A man who knew five languages well, Frank Schoonmaker spoke French "like a Frenchman, without a trace of an American accent," Jacques d'Angerville told me. "Frank was a generous man, very nice to the *vignerons*. He was also a good friend of many of the great restaurateurs of his time," said the current marquis, a soft-spoken, diffident man who went to work for Schoonmaker in 1960 and who today still runs the family's domaine in Volnay.

Sam Aaron, co-owner of Sherry-Lehmann, the carriage-trade wineshop in New York that began as Sherry Wine & Spirits in 1934, recalls accompanying Frank Schoonmaker on a few of his buying trips to Burgundy after the war. "Frank was a zealot. He was the man who made estate-bottled Burgundies fashionable in America.

"Traveling with him was a great experience. He knew Burgundy like a native, so well that he could draw the plan of every village, and he often knew three generations of the vintners' families. Frank was a great believer in the *Crus* of the Côte d'Or. He felt village appellation wines could be ordinary, and he was willing to pay more for *Premier Cru* and *Grand Cru*. We'd visit a vintner and taste the village wine and Frank would say, 'What could you do for two francs more?' Never 'What can we get for less?'

"The vintner's eyes would light up and he would bring out his best. Frank not only got good wines, he got good values. He'd say to me, 'You know, any moron can find a good bottle of wine for twenty dollars. It takes a genius to find one at five dollars.' My wineshop was Frank's biggest customer in his early days. I was buying at least fifty percent of his estate-bottled Burgundies then.

"Frank was a man of high intelligence and very great taste," Sam Aaron continued, in his gravel-grained voice and street-smart New York accent. "You know, there's usually one outstanding man you remember in each field. Picasso in art. Einstein in science. Freud in psychoanalysis. In wine, it's Schoonmaker. There could only be one Frank Schoonmaker in my lifetime."

William Leedom went to work for Frank Schoonmaker in 1969. Although he traveled with his employer on buying trips to Burgundy, Leedom's main work for Schoonmaker was in Germany. "As you know, Frank spoke many languages well, but he never really mastered German. When we were tasting wines together in Germany, I'd do the interpreting, and he was pretty impatient with the formalities. He kept saying, 'That's fine, that's fine, but let's get down to the tasting.' When we were tasting together in Burgundy, though, Frank would just go on. My French was like Frank's German, but he would get so involved, he'd never stop to interpret.

"He had a fabulous memory for wines. There were many winemakers in Germany who told me they felt Schoonmaker had the finest palate of anyone they had ever known. Frank was also known for his volatile temper. And he never brooked fools or nonsense," added Leedom, who worked for him until Schoonmaker's death, and then went on to become the U.S. agent for Graham's and Dow Ports and Philipponnat Champagne.

"When Frank read or heard people describe wines in pretentious terms, that temper would show. 'Pencil shavings,' I remember him saying once when he read a writer's description of a wine. 'What the hell do pencil shavings taste like?'

"He felt wines could be described in a few straight words.

One day, I remember, a few of us were in his office when someone brought in a very special bottle—a Bordeaux First Growth
close to thirty years old. The bottle was opened and poured, and
we all tasted. It was extraordinary. Superb. But no one said a
word. We all waited for Frank to make the first pronouncement.
He tasted for a while, and then he spoke: 'Well, that's some glass
of *vino*.'"

When Frank Schoonmaker died in 1976, at the age of seventy, he left behind much of his knowledge of wine in his books
and articles. And he instilled much of his passion for fine Burgundies in people who—each in his own way—carried on his quest
for the best of Burgundy.

One of his most passionate disciples was Alexis Lichine, a man
who in his more than fifty years in the wine trade has been at one
time or another, and often simultaneously, author, lecturer, retailer, importer, exporter, vintner, buyer and seller. Born in
Russia, brought up chiefly in Paris, he settled in the United States
soon after the repeal of Prohibition. His first job in wine was as
a salesman in a wineshop; his second was with the new wine
department of Saccone, Speed & Jenny importers. In that job, he
visited restaurants and wineshops in Manhattan, and before long
he counted among his fine wineshop customers Sherry Wine &
Spirits and M. Lehmann. In 1938, Lichine joined Frank Schoonmaker in his new importing firm, and a year later, Schoonmaker
sent him off to France to learn how to buy wine under the
instruction of Raymond Baudouin. When the United States entered the war, Lichine entered the U.S. Army.

"Soon after I became a civilian again, I returned to Burgundy," Lichine said. He was working on his own by then,
buying for wineshops, Sherry Wine & Spirits among them; and,
later, buying for New York's Waldorf-Astoria Hotel and for
Antoine's, the renowned restaurant in New Orleans. His mis-
sion, he says, was essentially the same as when he worked for
Schoonmaker: "To discover fine small growers and convince the
best of them to age and bottle their own wine. When I started
after the war, very few growers did that. By the fifties, about 7
to 10 percent were doing so.

"It was difficult work. I'd go from door to door with my
tasting cup in hand. They'd recognize me. My notoriety had

spread. And there would be great jealousy. Who was I buying from? they'd wonder. Who was I *not* buying from?"

An elegant man just over six feet tall, with a touch of gray in his dark, slicked-back hair, Lichine today shows only a bit of weariness in his face and none—absolutely none—in his enthusiasm for wine and in his memories of what Burgundy was nearly forty years ago. "I was begging them in Burgundy to bottle. I was begging them in the States to buy. I was fighting to get people to understand what real Burgundy was all about, that it was a far cry from what most *négociant-*shippers were sending to them. In those years, many *négociants* had the habit of substituting one appellation for another in their blends. You can understand why the shippers began to resent me more and more.

"The first time Sam Aaron went to Burgundy—around the mid-1950s—he was impressed with the difficulties involved in talking these people into estate bottling. Sam understood the whole scene."

Lichine sent the wine he chose back to America through H. Seymour Weller, a Milwaukee-born naturalized French citizen who was then manager of Château Haut-Brion in Bordeaux's Graves district and head of a shipping company. That arrangement continued until 1955, when Lichine, by then the owner of his own château in Bordeaux, established Alexis Lichine & Co. as a French exporting firm located in Margaux, and an importing firm, also under his name, in the United States. He sold the controlling interest in his export company in the 1960s, and though the name continues—through still another owner—the wines, he is quick to point out, no longer represent Alexis Lichine because Alexis Lichine no longer selects the wines.

A couple of decades earlier, about the time Raymond Baudouin and Frank Schoonmaker had begun working together, there was an American in Paris named Henry Hollis. A former teetotaler and U.S. senator from Vermont, Henry Hollis first went to France on business, discovered wine, and stayed on for the rest of his life, pursuing his newborn interest. He quickly made up for his lost years as a nondrinker, and before long he was buying wines for American importers and wineshops. One of the people for whom he chose wine was Sidney Haas, who owned the fine wineshop M. Lehmann, Inc., in New York City.

The shop was named after Haas's uncle Moritz Lehmann, whose family had come to the United States from Alsace and who had been in the wine business before Prohibition. Haas had received the first independent wine and liquor license in New York State after repeal. It was numbered L-12, the first eleven licenses having gone to Macy's, Bloomingdale's and other department stores.

"We had the most prestigious customers," Sidney Haas says. "Governor Lehman—no relation—used to buy his wines from us. We had the reputation of knowing more about wine than any shop in the city—maybe in the country. Stores from other states used to send their salesmen to us for training."

Henry Hollis had helped supply Sidney Haas with the wines of Domaine de la Romanée-Conti, Marquis d'Angerville and Henri Gouges, among other Burgundies. Hollis introduced Haas to many people in France, including Raymond Baudouin. When Hollis died, soon after World War II, Haas asked Baudouin to buy for him in France. Baudouin died in 1953, and once again M. Lehmann was without a buyer. Sidney spoke no French, which did not stop him from recognizing the importance of estate-bottled Burgundy. His son Robert, who had joined him in the wineshop in 1950 after finishing college, was new to the wine trade, but he spoke a little French and showed a lot of enthusiasm. His father decided to send him on his first trip to France in April 1954, to find a new buyer.

"I couldn't find a good buyer," Bob says now, "but I fell in love with France, so I decided I would become the new buyer. I was totally without significant qualifications, you understand, but I started with Baudouin's suppliers in Burgundy and they would not let me go wrong. I'd taste and say, 'Yes, I'll take that barrel.' And they'd say, 'No, you don't want that barrel. You want this barrel.' You might say I learned on the job."

In 1955, Bob Haas opened a joint office with Frank Schoonmaker in Paris, and during those years he traveled through Burgundy, sometimes alone, sometimes with Schoonmaker. "I became more interested in importing and less in the retail part of the business, so my father sold our shop in 1961 to Joseph Stricks, who had been the store manager of Sherry Wine & Spirits. Sam Aaron and his brother Jack bought the shop in 1965 and merged it with theirs. And that's how Sherry-Lehmann came about."

Bob Haas formed his own firm, Leeds Distributors, Inc., in 1961; a few years later, he and Schoonmaker severed ties. Schoonmaker eventually sold his company to Pillsbury, which later sold it to its present owner, Joseph E. Seagram & Sons. Bob Haas also sold his company, to Barton Brands in Chicago, although he continued to work for the new owner for three years. After resigning in 1970, he moved to Vermont, where he opened a new import firm, Vineyard Brands. "When I started with Baudouin, he had about a half-dozen suppliers in Burgundy, and only about ten percent of the region's vintners bottled their own wine. Today, I represent twenty-six Burgundians who estate-bottle; and in the region as a whole, I estimate that about 60 percent of the reds and 30 to 35 percent of the whites are now bottled by the growers. When a vintner bottles under his own name, it involves a certain pride; he knows he must put something good in that bottle.

"Burgundy represents the largest single part of my import business—over 30 percent. There's so much truth in Burgundy. I guess that's why I'm still in love with the region."

Among other importers who helped in Burgundy's evolution toward estate bottling was Colonel Frederick Wildman. His interest in fine wine blossomed soon after World War I, when, as a young U.S. Army lieutenant stationed in Germany, he was told to go to the wine regions of Europe to buy wines for the officers' mess. He was in Burgundy, his son Freddy says, when Prohibition began in the United States.

Fourteen years later, as soon as Prohibition ended, Wildman and some friends bought Bellows & Co. and established what Freddy calls the first importing firm in this country dealing with fine wines.

The supply of those wines was cut drastically during World War II, and in the early 1940s, just before Colonel Frederick Wildman joined the U.S. Army Air Force, Bellows was sold to National Distillers.

In 1952, the colonel opened his own importing firm, Frederick Wildman & Sons, Ltd., with Freddy and two stepsons, Ned and Solon Kelley. Colonel Wildman had been importing Domaine de la Romanée-Conti's wines since the 1930s, when he was president of Bellows & Co. During the twenty years that his wine company remained in the family, it continued to import Domaine de la Romanée-Conti, as well as other fine Burgundies: Domaine Leflaive, Domaine Armand Rousseau and the *négociant* Louis Latour among them.

In 1971, the company was sold to Hiram Walker Gooderham & Worts, a Canadian-based company whose prime holdings are in spirits. Freddy stayed on for a few years and during that time added Domaine Dujac of Morey-Saint-Denis to the list of Burgundy imports. Six years later, he left Wildman. For some years he lived abroad, mostly in Spain, writing and traveling through wine country. In 1984, he formed his own company, F. Starr & Associates, operating from the family home in Colebrook, Connecticut. (Starr is his middle name.) And so Frederick Starr Wildman, who remembers going to Burgundy on a wine-buying trip with his parents in 1936, when he was six years old, is back in the wine business, searching out wines in the United States and in Europe, and especially in Burgundy.

Since the early 1960s, Warren Strauss has also encouraged Burgundy's estate bottlers, bringing to the United States such suppliers as Roland Rapet of Pernand-Verglesses, Hubert Lemy of Saint-Aubin and Bernard Drouhin of Domaine Drouhin-Laroze in Gevrey-Chambertin.

The British wine trade had no one person involved in Burgundy's estate bottling movement who was the equal of Frank Schoonmaker or Alexis Lichine. Mostly, the British part of the story involves firms rather than individuals. There was Heyman Brothers, which as early as the 1930s brought the wines of Armand Rousseau, Henri Gouges and Roland Thévenin to Great Britain. Some of the wines of Domaine de la Romanée-Conti and the Marquis d'Angerville were also there in the thirties. Soon after World War II, Averys of Bristol bought the wines of Comte de Vogüé and Louis Poirier, among others. And in the late 1960s, Leonard and Stanley Dennis, brothers who worked for Grants of Saint James's, brought in still other estate-bottled Burgundies. They and others—French, American and British— helped establish the small grower-bottler of Burgundy.

Yet curiously, despite the great role played by the wine trade of the United States, until Rebecca Wasserman began Le Serbet in 1979, there had never been an American wine broker who dealt with the small estate bottler, who encouraged growers and worked with them and who at the same time lived permanently in Burgundy, only minutes from most growers, never more than an hour away from any of them.

11

LE SERBET GROWS

Like the people who preceded her in the estate bottling evolution, Becky Wasserman had to work hard in two directions. In Burgundy, she had to find producers whose wines were of the quality she sought. In the United States, she had to find importers who would be willing to handle wines from *vignerons* most of whose names they did not know.

"In the beginning, I found suppliers through a lot of different sources. Aubert de Villaine, for example, introduced me to many people on the Côte Chalonnaise. Other friends introduced me to people in Saint-Aubin and other wine villages.

"Sometimes I would start by choosing a wine that interested me. Let's say I wanted a wine from Savigny-lès-Beaune. I'd go through the telephone book and make a list of every producer in the village. It was as basic as that. I might have tasted a vintner's wine in a restaurant. Or someone might have told me about him. Or I had been thinking about that domaine for a long time. Or I might not know his wines at all and decide I wanted to taste them so that I would know them.

"By one method or another, I'd arrive at Savigny-lès-Beaune. I'd taste seriously, usually in the cellar. In my early days, I used to be immediately, emotionally committed. Now I can tell pretty quickly if I'm interested, but I don't make an immediate commitment."

Finding the wines she liked was the first step. Then came other considerations. Did she want to work with this vintner? Would he like to export? Did he already have an exporter? If he agreed to have Becky as his agent, she would then reserve a small quantity of his wine for a limited time, explain her system to him, and if he hadn't exported before, tell him how he must print his labels to conform to American federal laws for alcoholic beverages.

"A label change may seem like an insignificant thing, but in Burgundy, where many label machines are not adjustable, it means adding a strip label by hand. I always supply the strip, but it can still loom as a major problem. Sometimes it seems so big that a *vigneron* who has never exported before may refuse to start. The heavy paperwork involved in exporting could also be a stumbling block."

Whatever other difficulties Becky may have encountered in starting her brokerage, being accepted as an American in France was not one of them. "Curiously, no *vigneron* questioned that. I assume it's because I had lived in Burgundy so long," she said.

As Becky went from village to village, from *vigneron* to *vigneron*, she would find that for every ten growers she visited, perhaps one would have the kind of wines she felt were worthy. "They were the wines I was looking for, the best of breed."

With a small portfolio of well-chosen wines, Becky then had to find importers in the United States. Diamond Wine Merchants had been her beginning. And a Saint-Aubin Blanc 1975 made by André Thomas was the first wine she sent her first client.

For a while, Becky was also an agent for Kermit Lynch of California. Lynch had been dealing directly with small producers throughout France, and he had encountered problems trying to organize shipments of these wines to the United States.

As his agent, Becky had to consolidate his wines, see that they were collected from producers in different regions of the country, packed in the same container and shipped to California.

"I learned a lot about that side of the business working for Kermit. I also learned to appreciate Kermit's reaction to a really good wine—the way he never bruised one moment of enjoyment by analyzing and comparing that wine. He would just leave the moment alone and not spoil it."

After this start came the hard and gritty work. "I would go to the United States, traveling from city to city. I would walk around, browsing through wineshops to see what was available, eating in restaurants so that I could study their wine lists. I traveled alone, taking night flights because they were cheaper, staying in cheap hotels. I had absolutely no idea what I was doing; I just did what seemed logical. My constant question to retailers and restaurateurs was: 'Why? Why not try wines from lesser-known estates?' I was very scared, but I was so convinced of the quality of the wines I was selling that I thought all obstacles were surmountable."

In those first years, there were some rude encounters. "I remember one retailer particularly, in New York," Becky said. "I had an appointment; I had reconfirmed it. When I went to the shop, I was told to wait. When I was finally allowed to speak to the owner, he started by saying, 'I will give you one minute only. Do you understand? One minute.'

" 'I've come from France to talk to you,' I said. 'I reconfirmed my appointment with you.' He sneered. 'Who are you anyway?' I made up my mind right then that I would never treat anyone in this business that way. That's why Le Serbet has always been open, why we welcome every serious wine professional who comes to visit."

Slowly, doors did open and people did listen; Becky found importers in Chicago, Washington State, Michigan, Boston, New York City and, in time, other cities and states, as well.

Slowly, too, she found the Burgundies she liked and vintners with whom she wanted to work. Prestigious domaines began to join her. Philippe de Magenta, whom she had known since her days in Saint-Romain, became a supplier. Gérard Potel of Pousse d'Or in Volnay began to work with Le Serbet. At the same time, she was discovering *vignerons* who were less known and who came from less-known appellations, and she worked with them, helping and encouraging until they were able to finish and bottle their own wine.

An example is Alain Gras of Saint-Romain. Now a young man in his twenties, he was a youngster Becky knew slightly during the years she lived in the village. In 1979, after her wine brokerage was established, she stopped by one day to taste his wines out of barrel before he sold them off to a *négociant*. Becky liked them and convinced him to keep some of the wine back. If he would age and bottle it himself, she said, she would help him sell it.

"I needed that much of a push," cherubic-faced Alain Gras said. "I had always been sad to see my wines taken away to the *négociant.* We worked so hard to grow those grapes and bring them in and make the wine. So even before Becky, I knew there had to be more than just watching my wines leave for someone else's label."

Saint-Romain is a small village and a small appellation, and in the past, Alain said, much of it would be sold under the regional Bourgogne appellation rather than under the village's own appellation. A wine can be classified down—in this case, from village down to regional. It can never be classified up.

Alain Gras farms about twelve acres in Saint-Romain and in Auxey-Duresses. Five of those acres were given to him by his father, René, as unplanted land, along with a house on the rim of the land. He planted; he bought a bit more land; and he also works other acreage, under the *métayage* system.

In *métayage,* a worker such as Alain Gras farms the land for its owner, and the two share the fruit. While the percentage may vary with the individual arrangement, the person working the vineyards usually keeps one half to two thirds, with the rest going to the owner. Generally, the land's owner buys the vines. The worker provides the tractor and other machinery. A *métayage* contract runs for a minimum of nine years, although each side retains the right to cancel the contract, giving advance notice, every one and a half to three years, depending on the agreement.

Under Becky's tutelage, Alain Gras has moved in a very few years from selling 100 percent of his production to *négociants* to bottling 100 percent of his own production. That adds up to about twenty thousand bottles a year under the Alain Gras label. The village produces more white than red, and the Gras production is mostly in white.

For years, Becky had been honing her tasting ability. But whereas once it was a pleasurable avocation, now, as a professional, she worked as though life depended on it. And in a very real way, the life of her company did depend on it.

Tasting wine is a matter of using one's senses—sight, smell and taste. While all three senses enter into an evaluation of wine, smell is the first major clue to a wine's quality. In that sense,

Becky earns her living with her nose. "I've been smelling seriously all my life," she said. "As a myopic child, smell was very
important to me. I smelled everything intensely. I loved the
smell of burning leaves, all foods, even the smell of New York
City buses.

"In wine, the first thing I look for is flaws, which I can find
more readily by smell than by taste. That's true for me whether
the wine is in cask or bottle. White wines are particularly sensitive to such things as oxidation and unclean cellar conditions. So
first I check a wine's state of health.

"I then sniff to see if the appellation characteristics are recog-
nizable. There is general agreement in the wine trade about how
a particular wine should smell. We also agree that the lesser
white wines of Burgundy can sometimes offer more in youth
than greater wines do. A young village Meursault, for example,
generally displays more bouquet than a *Premier Cru.* But it is not
the most evident bouquet in the beginning that will necessarily
be the greater wine in the end.

"Next comes aroma, which for me is linked to personal defi-
nitions. Here, I analyze the wine, take it apart in my mind, think
about what it reminds me of—roses, hazelnuts. Smell is Prous-
tian, an evocative kind of thing. Bouquet is the last step. I think
of it as the total impression, one that I don't want to break up
into parts. Tasting—and by that, I refer to the whole process of
observing and smelling and tasting—is working hard, with all the
senses turned on. But the professional part doesn't preclude the
sensual pleasure. There have been many times when we've tasted
in this intensely analytical way all day. We were exhausted. But
introduce some exciting new wines in the evening, and I'm
absolutely thrilled. I wouldn't miss trying them for anything."

In 1980, Robert Finigan, the San Francisco–based editor and
publisher of the monthly newsletter *Private Guide to Wines,* introduced Becky to Christopher Cannan, a young Englishman who
operated a wine brokerage firm called Europvin in Bordeaux.
Like Becky, he looked for the undiscovered and the best of
breed. Christopher Cannan's wines were mostly from Bordeaux,
with some from the Loire and a few from other regions. He had

only a few wines from Burgundy, and he sold chiefly to European markets. Becky, on the other hand, had no Bordeaux wines, and she sold principally in the United States.

"On my next trip to the States, I took Christopher's list, and I came back with orders for him. We decided to work together but to remain separate companies. It's worked well. We issue a joint list of our wines under the name Cannan & Wasserman; and Christopher's office, which has a computer, handles the administration work."

With a stronger base, Becky began to look into other French wine regions—Côtes du Rhône, Champagne, the Midi—and Christopher Cannan began to enlarge his territory, moving into other parts of France and into Spain.

Meanwhile, Becky continued to build her Burgundy collection, adding such domaines as Philippe Rossignol and Alain Burguet, both in Gevrey-Chambertin, Vadey Castagnier in Morey-Saint-Denis; Daniel Rion & Fils in Vosne-Romanée; and André Mussy in Pommard.

By 1985, the Cannan & Wasserman list included nearly fifty Burgundy estates. Together with wines from other parts of France and from Spain, it represented more than 250 estates. And the two companies export jointly to the United States, Great Britain, Holland, Japan, Australia, Canada, Hong Kong, Singapore and New Zealand.

One day in 1981, Count René Lafon of Meursault, who had met Becky earlier at a wine tasting, telephoned. His oldest son, Dominique, was about to finish military service; would it be possible for Becky to get him a job with a winery in California? Dominique had studied agricultural engineering in Dijon for a year and then attended the two-year course at the Lycée Agricole et Viticole de Beaune. He graduated when he was twenty-two years old, and had worked in a wineshop in the south of France for a short time before starting his compulsory year in the army. Mel Knox was visiting Becky at the time of Count Lafon's call, and the two of them went to lunch at the Lafon domaine, to meet Dominique. Mel and Becky spoke to him in English to see how much of the language he understood, but the handsome young man with sharply chiseled Gallic features was very quiet.

"I felt so bad," he says now. "I had been stationed in Germany for my year in the military and I had been speaking German. What English I learned in school had disappeared. I couldn't speak and I kept saying to myself, 'I've got to make it. This is my chance.' But I was stumbling all over. Then, to make everything worse, my father served our Montrachet in water glasses—not wineglasses. The glasses are hundred-year-old crystal, and that's how we are used to serving wine in Burgundy, but I was quite upset. 'Please,' I asked my family, 'can't we have wineglasses for the Montrachet?' Maybe that helped. Anyway, with Mel's help, I got a job in California at the J. W. Morris Winery."

Dominique found life in California wonderful. "I loved the climate, the music, the people. What I liked most about the people there is that they are self-starters, willing to try new things. I was also very impressed with the machinery and the equipment in the wineries, and with the cleanliness.

"California was the first place I had ever tasted such a range of wines. There were California wines, yes, but also wines from Spain and Italy, from all over the world. I even tasted French wines in California that I had not had in France.

"But there were also things that surprised me—for example, I was disappointed to find there were no underground cellars, as we have in Burgundy. And I was surprised to hear some small wineries, which had never before made wine, talk about making wine in the style of Domaine de la Romanée-Conti when they did not know what the Domaine style was all about. Even if they had known, there's no way to copy a winemaking system when the climate, the soil, everything, is different.

"There were times in California when I felt so fortunate to be born in Burgundy and to have the chance to look at Burgundy from the outside."

Dominique Lafon returned to France six months later, speaking English and happy for the experience, but also happy to be back. "Personally, I loved California, but oenologically, California did not change me."

On his return, Dominique stopped by Le Serbet to tell Becky about his trip. Before long, he was working for her part-time, doing such chores as organizing her wine cellar, while he looked for a job.

That lasted two weeks. On October 1982, he began to work full-time for Le Serbet. "Becky never really outlined the job or told me exactly what I would be doing," says Dominique.

It was soon clear what he could do for Le Serbet. As a trained taster, he helped choose wines. As an oenologist, he could identify a problem in a wine, do the laboratory analysis and explain to the producer what was wrong. As a personable young Burgundian, he was able to help find other producers for Le Serbet.

"I hear about good producers from other people, from friends, especially from young winemakers about my own age; or we find new wines at public tastings and on local restaurant lists," Dominique says.

One of Dominique's young winemaker friends is Frédéric Lafarge, who works with his father, Michel Lafarge, at the family domaine in Volnay. From the time she began Le Serbet, Becky had wanted Michel Lafarge to be one of her suppliers. "I knew his wines were excellent. And I heard he was a very fine man. But I also knew he was rather stern and I found it hard to approach him. One day, though, I just called. I said I'd like to bring an American client over to meet him and to taste. Michel wasn't really eager to export to the United States. And I had to tell him how important it was that the better wines of Burgundy be available to consumers there. Finally, he let me export the first few cases."

He has stayed with Le Serbet since, and he is one of the shining glories on the list. His domaine and his family symbolize so much that is good and lasting in Burgundy—the tradition that stretches back as far as memory and, at the same time, the continuity that will carry on into new generations.

12

THE LAFARGES:

TRADITION AND THE VINEYARDS

❦

Volnay is a wine village that long ago settled comfortably into its own tradition. Seasons, years, generations pass; good harvests and poor harvests pass; and the land continues to play out its annual cycle while its people continue to step into the future with an ear turned to catch the lessons of the past.

Here, on Rue de la Combe, one of the narrow streets that radiate out from Place de l'Église, the village square, live Michel Lafarge, his wife, Noëlle, and their four children.

Michel Lafarge was born in Volnay on November 9, 1928, in the house next to and now attached to his present home. Like his father and grandfather and all his family as far back as his great-great-great-grandfather, who was born before the French Revolution, Michel Lafarge is a *vigneron*. Since 1983, Michel Lafarge is also the mayor of this village of 450 inhabitants, just as his father and his grandfather had been. When he was eighteen years old, he began to work with his father in the family's vineyards and winery. When Michel's older son, Frédéric, was nineteen years old, he began to work with his father in the family's vineyards and winery.

If it has been the fate of Burgundy to have its vineyards chipped into mosaic patterns, it has also been its fate to be secured by custom and family. And few families portray this continuity more clearly than the Lafarges.

Michel Lafarge is a strong, ruggedly attractive man with blue eyes that send out warm signals even when he is looking his sternest, and with hair that had been pale blond before it began turning white when he was thirty. He is a man of quiet authority, in command in his vineyards and winery and village and in his family. When he smiles, which he does often, it is a benign smile that deepens the creases embedded by a lifetime spent in the vineyards.

When his father, Henri, died in 1967, he left nine hectares, or 22¼ acres, to be divided among his three sons. If all of the brothers had been *vignerons,* each would have worked his own three hectares and made his own wine and perhaps would have looked for other property to buy or to work under the *métayage* system. But neither of Michel's brothers wanted to be a *vigneron;* one is the manager of a plastics firm, the other the director of a wine distribution company in the city of Lyon.

And so Michel slowly bought back from his two brothers their part of the inheritance. To the nine hectares he later added another hectare, bringing his total to ten hectares, or 24.7 acres, a good-sized property by Burgundy standards. Five and a half of the hectares are in Volnay, both in the village appellation and in two *Premier Cru* vineyards. Three-quarters of a hectare is in the *Premier Cru* vineyard Beaune-Grèves. One hectare is in Meursault. And the remaining 2¾ hectares are in vineyards of Appellation Contrôlée Bourgogne—Bourgogne Aligoté and Bourgogne Passetoutgrains, which Michel Lafarge produces with 50 percent Pinot Noir, 50 percent Gamay. As is done for many Passetoutgrains, the grapes are planted in the blend's proportion within the same vineyard.

"Today, it would be very difficult to buy our vineyards—and very expensive," Michel Lafarge said. "In Burgundy, we still use an old measure called an *ouvrée.* An *ouvrée* is 428 square meters, so there are between 23 and 24 *ouvrées* in one hectare. In the newspapers you will see advertised so many *ouvrées* for sale; and that is what people buy—three, four, five *ouvrées.* It is rare to buy a whole hectare now."

Like many Burgundians, the Lafarge family live above their wine cellars: Michel and Noëlle; their two daughters—pretty, red-haired Anne-Françoise, who is a student at the University of Dijon, and blond, vivacious Cecile, who was born fourteen years ago on Christmas Day, her mother's birthday; and their two sons —Benoît, who is studying engineering, and Frédéric, who studied viticulture and oenology.

Their home reflects the family, neat and proper and friendly, with a large, square kitchen brightened by splashes of blue; and across the back of the house, a living room and dining room decorated in green, gold and beige. From the windows of these two rooms, one looks out on the gentle slope behind the house that is the Lafarges' Volnay *Premier Cru* vineyard, called Le Village.

When Michel Lafarge bought the house next door to his parents' home, he cut a doorway between them, so that the two now connect. For most of the year, the house of his parents is used only for storage. But come autumn, twenty or more pickers arrive, and the old house becomes a dormitory for ten, twelve, sometimes fifteen days, depending on how long the harvest lasts that year.

In the mid-1970s, Michel Lafarge had new *caves* dug under his house. Like the two houses, the new *caves* connect to old ones, so that the Lafarge cellars now range in age from about ten years to those dug out in the twelfth century, *caves* with rounded ceilings so low that even the shortest of us must duck to go under its archways.

The smells of the Lafarge cellars are wonderful, a mingling of aromas of wines from different vineyards and of different ages, of the smell of moist earth and rock, with hints of the original fruit of the vine. Like all good Burgundian cellars, the walls are thick with fungus that thrives on humidity and the presence of wine in cask.

Here at Lafarge, there are wines made of Pinot Noir, of Chardonnay, of Aligoté and Gamay. And for the *vigneron*, each must be treated differently. "Pinot Noir is the most fragile, the most sensitive of the four, and it needs the most care. Chardonnay can also be fragile, but generally not as much as Pinot Noir. Aligoté is easier because it is more robust. And Gamay tends to be more like Aligoté in vigor," Michel explained.

We were tasting his Volnay 1982, still in cask, a lovely wine with the aroma of raspberries and a very pretty color—*"une belle robe,"* as the French call it.

Was this a typical Volnay?

He nodded. "Volnay has a great deal of bouquet, and it is floral, very feminine, very elegant. It can be drunk when it is young, and can also age."

The Lafarge family. From left to right, Anne-Françoise, Michel, Benoît, Cecile, Frédéric and Nöelle.

Gérard Potel of Domaine Pousse d'Or, a neighbor and close friend of the Lafarges, was tasting with us. "For me, a typical Volnay shows the wonderful character of Pinot Noir," Monsieur Potel said. "It has finesse. It can be hard, but the fruit must be very elegant. When a Volnay ages, the bouquet becomes very complex."

Burgundy seems always to have recognized the nobility of the Pinot Noir.

In old notebooks that Noëlle Lafarge showed me one day, there were records of the family's wine sales dating back to the mid-1800s. "If a barrel of Gamay was sold, it is listed as a barrel of Gamay," she said. "But wherever it says 'a barrel of *bon vin*,'" it means a barrel of Pinot Noir. Here you see 'Passetoutgrains,' and here, *'vin blanc.'* The family did not yet own the vineyard in Meursault."

As early as the 1850s, Michel's great-grandfather was selling wine in barrel to restaurants. By 1860, the notebooks show, he was shipping wine in barrel to Paris. By the time the century had turned, the family had sold its first wine in bottle. "It was in 1906," Noëlle continued, "and the wine was from the 1904 harvest. It cost four gold francs a bottle." Bottles of this wine, from 1904, the oldest wine the family has, still rest in the Lafarge cellars.

Beginning with the 1934 vintage, Michel's father began to sell much more wine in bottle to restaurants and to special people in Paris. And by the late 1930s, he had begun to export to Switzerland and Belgium. World War II halted that. The Germans came to Burgundy in 1940, and Michel's father was forced to house them. "They went into our *caves* and drank our best wines—three hundred bottles of our 1915, and other wines, as well. They knew which ones to take because my father had put the vintages on the bottles. Since then, we have never marked our bottles with their years. I remember, too, that my mother had to ask the Germans for permission to go into her own kitchen to heat food for my brothers and me." Michel was a student in those years; he says very little more about the Germans.

After the war, when the village returned to normal, Henri Lafarge was elected mayor of Volnay, an office he held for twenty years. In 1946, Michel finished school and began to work with his father.

"Actually, I always worked with my father, since I was very young. I grew up learning and knowing what the wines of Volnay were. I remember the details of every vintage since 1937. I was just a boy then, only nine years old, but I remember it. In fact, 1937 is still my favorite wine."

What other vintages does Michel Lafarge favor? "Many, many. After 1937, I would say I particularly like 1945, 1959, 1961, 1969, 1978 and 1983."

If these were the best, what were the worst? "Nineteen sixty —big quantity but very bad quality; 1975 was also very bad. But perhaps 1956 was the worst. I needed only four pickers that year; there were very few grapes, and they made very poor wine."

The year 1956 may have been bad in the vineyards, but it was good in other ways for Michel Lafarge, for it was the year he married Noëlle Renaud.

Benoît grew up liking wine, but never, he says, as much as his older brother. Frédéric, on the other hand, always wanted to be a *vigneron.* "Since I was a little boy, I wanted to be with my father in the vineyards and the winery and to ask him about everything he was doing."

Tell Michel Lafarge that his daughters are beautiful, that his children are bright and well mannered, that his family is wonderful, and he smiles that warm, quiet smile and says, "Yes, I know."

Growing up enveloped in tradition, the Lafarges have remained loyal to that tradition. Anne-Françoise and Benoît spend weekdays at their schools, but they return to Volnay each weekend. With the Lafarges, lunch and dinner are always family affairs. And so, in fact, are vacations. They take two each year and they take them together.

"We go away in August because there is not as much to do in the vineyards and because we never ship wine then; it's too hot," Michel said, "and we take a week in February."

"Oh, Papa, please let's show her the films," Cecile said.

We watched films of their vacations—sledding down a snowy slope in the Jura Mountains, riding on a carousel in Germany. And then we watched another film—one of Noëlle and Michel

[85]

with Françoise and Gérard Potel and Becky Wasserman when the five of them went to the United States in 1983.

They visited Texas and Boston and San Francisco. They went to Oregon, where Pete Stern, who is a wine retailer in Chicago, and his wife, Florence, joined them. Oregon planted Pinot Noir and Chardonnay, the noble grapes of Burgundy, only about twenty years ago, and Michel Lafarge was particularly eager to see what the new winegrowers had done with these grapes.

Was Oregon wine country interesting? "Yes."

Are the Oregonians making good wine? "Yes."

Did you learn anything new about grape growing or wine-making? "Perhaps."

Has it affected the way you do things here now? "No."

In Burgundy, tradition prevails.

It is both tradition and the natural cycle of the vine that determines what must be done in the vineyards each month. The year's work begins after the festival of Saint Vincent, the patron saint of *vignerons,* which takes place the third week of January. The vines are dormant then, empty of sap and impervious to all but the most extreme frost. It is at this time that Michel and Frédéric start the *taille,* the pruning, which consists of cutting off much of the previous year's growth—canes and shoots, for example—and cutting back the number of buds, or *yeux* (eyes), as the French call them, to limit the crop of grapes in the next harvest to fewer, top-quality clusters.

There are three methods of training vines. In the Côte d'Or, the most commonly used method is the Guyot cordon. Training a vine in its early life establishes how the vine's growth will be directed, and gives a certain form to the permanent parts of the vine. Pruning is the cutting back of the vine to maintain that form and symmetry and to control its growth. In the Guyot cordon, the vine is kept low, with only one branch retained each year and with six buds left on that branch. A second, shorter branch is kept to prepare for the following year.

From one bud, or *bourgeon,* one shoot will grow, and that shoot in turn may produce one, two or, at most, three clusters of grapes as well as leaves. If too many buds are left, the vine may not have the energy to bring all the clusters to maturity, or if they do ripen, they may not be of the highest quality. If too few buds are left, the quality may be high but the yield will be especially small. In deciding how many buds to leave, the *vigneron* must also consider the growth pattern of each variety, the age of each vine and its past yields.

During February and sometimes into March, the Lafarges continue the *taille,* vine by vine, day after day. February is also the time they plant a few new vines and replace any of last year's new vines that did not take.

Perhaps in March, sometimes in April, depending on the weather and if the soil is dry, plowing begins. While the vines are still dormant, Michel and Frédéric also begin the first of many treatments to protect against the diseases, parasites and insects that can attack and often destroy the vines. It is in March, too, that the Lafarges fasten the branch of the vine to the bottom wire, one of the three horizontal wires stretched one above the other and secured to wood posts.

Michel and Frédéric may continue to plow throughout April. In those places between vines where the mechanical plow cannot reach, they break up the earth by hand, with a flat iron plate attached to a long handle, called a *fessou* in Burgundian dialect. The vines are given another treatment, this one to prevent acariasis, infestation by mites that penetrate the vine through either the wood or the leaves, causing deformation of the leaves.

Throughout the months of vineyard work—until harvest—the Lafarges generally work from 7 A.M. to noon, from 1:30 to 6 P.M.

"The principal concern of May is the weather," Michel Lafarge said one rainy May evening in 1984. "You must try to forecast it and adapt to it. Today, for example, the morning was beautiful and the soil dry after all the rains. So we used this time to give the vines a treatment against mildew and oïdium. Just looking at the sky, I knew it would rain by this evening. And now you see, outside, how it is pouring. We will treat for these two problems again in June and July. We do it five to ten times in a growing season, depending on the year and the situation. This year, while we've had so much rain and it is very humid, it is also cold. That makes the wetness less dangerous than if it were warm."

Early May is also the time when the threat of hailstorms begins, and it does not end until the fall. A particular peril in Burgundy, these storms of hard little balls of ice and snow rip across the land in an erratic path, scarring, weakening, devastating one vineyard with the fury of exploding bullets while sparing another vineyard close by. In 1968, the Lafarges were spared not by vineyard location but by time. "Hail hit the day after our harvest was completed." But they were hit badly in August of 1971, when about sixty percent of that year's crop was destroyed.

And Michel Lafarge still remembers how drastically Volnay was struck in 1945, with more than 90 percent of the harvest devastated. In 1979, on the other hand, they were spared, while many vineyards in Nuits-Saint-Georges and Vosne-Romanée lost almost 100 percent of their grapes. And in 1983, at least 50 percent of the crop was lost again in the same two communes, as well as in Chambolle-Musigny.

Thunderstorms can also be severe in Burgundy. "In '82, there was an especially bad thunderstorm, and in 1975 and 1969 too." These storms bring tremendous amounts of water, which washes away the soil, channeling out deep furrows in the earth.

After pruning is completed, and before hailstorms and thunderstorms become a threat, comes the awakening of the vine. Beginning usually in April, occasionally later, in the time of spring when the temperatures begin to rise to a daily average of 50 degrees Fahrenheit, the sap in the dormant vine flows again. The buds swell until they push aside the scales that have enclosed and protected them during the winter, and they burst out, small, round and fuzzy. This is bud break, *l'éclatement de bourgeon,* the first stage of the new cycle. The vines experience a great surge of growth now, sending out leaves along the young shoots. It is in the leaves that photosynthesis takes place, a process by which a plant, using the sun as the source of energy, converts carbon dioxide and water into carbohydrates, which then travel through the vines to the grapes.

The vines are growing fast, and in disorder, and it is time for the *ébourgeonnement,* or second pruning, the trimming away of excess buds and foliage to ensure the quality of the harvest. Flower clusters soon form along the shoots. Each cluster is topped with tiny blossoms, and each blossom in the cluster is covered with a cap. When the cap falls away, usually in late spring, the flowering parts of the vine are exposed and fertilization takes place. Nearly all vinifera vines are hermaphroditic—that is, they contain both female and male organs. The pistil, or female, is composed of a stigma, a style and, at the bottom, an ovary; the four stamens that surround the pistil are threadlike growths topped with anthers that bear pollen.

When the pollen is discharged, tiny grains of it are caught by the stigma, situated at the top of the pistil. They germinate there, growing down the slender style into the ovary, where fertilization takes place. Soon after fertilization, the clusters of berries are set.

Before the flowering, however, as the vines grow taller, Michel and Frédéric put them between the middle wire, which is double, and fasten the wires together with *agrafes,* small metal hooks; in this way, the vines will be supported and grow straight.

How long the vines will be in flower depends on the year. "In 1983, it lasted five days because the weather was very hot," Michel Lafarge said as he clasped the wires together with an *agrafe.* "Usually, it lasts eight days."

In 1984, after a warm April, the weather remained cold and wet throughout May and into early June, and flowering was late, taking place the third week of June. Weather is especially important during flowering. In order to set properly, the vines need warm, sunny days free of rain and strong wind. If the weather isn't benign, many of the flowers, flower clusters or new berries will not develop well or will simply drop off the vine.

By the end of flowering, the new berries are formed—tiny, green and hard. Michel and Frédéric go through the vineyards doing the first *rognage,* clipping excess foliage to encourage berry development rather than that of leaf and wood.

If the weather is bad during flowering, if the set is bad, the berries few or small, it means a small crop. "But it affects quan-

[89]

tity, not quality," Michel Lafarge said. "In 1969, for example, the flowering was very late and bad, and the harvest was late, but the quality of the wine was very good. The year 1978 was very much like 1969. The weather was bad for flowering. The quantity of the grapes was low and the harvest was late—in October. But the quality was high. The year 1976, however, was very precocious, with the harvest beginning September 6. And it was a very good year. September and October are the most important part of the year's growth period; they are the months that determine quality. No one can know that quality until the harvest. Even during harvest, we do not know the exact quality. Last year, 1984, is a perfect example," he said with a smile, one day in February of 1985. "It turned out better than I expected."

The harvest usually begins about one hundred days after the flowering. "And a great deal happens in that time," Michel Lafarge reminded me. "There is more plowing in June and July. There is the second *rognage* in July. At the end of August, we give the vines the last treatment against disease, and particularly against berry rot if weather conditions are adverse."

The *véraison* occurs in August, the stage when the grapes change color from young green to yellow and then evolve toward their final shade of golden yellow for Chardonnay, deep blue for Pinot Noir, just before harvest. "The new young vines need a great deal of attention," Michel said. "And the vines need a great deal of sun, but of course, that is one thing we cannot arrange. We can only hope."

After *véraison,* the grapes enter their final maturing stage. At this point, the concentration of acids in the grapes is at its maximum. The balance of acids within the grape will change, however. In the beginning of the season, the levels of tartaric and malic acids are almost equal. By harvest, under normal conditions, the total acidity is more likely to be about 75 percent tartaric acid, 20 percent malic acid and 5 percent fruit acids.

At the same time, the sugar content begins to rise. While the grapes are developing sugar, they are also undergoing an enormous spurt of growth, becoming plump with juice; as a result, the proportion of acid to sugar decreases.

The *vigneron* watches the grapes carefully now and prepares for the harvest. He hopes for warm, dry days. Heavy rains at this

Michel and Frédéric Lafarge putting the vines between the double middle wire and fastening the wires together with *agrafes*.

time can lower quality. Cold weather can keep the grapes from ripening fully, so that the sugar level remains low and acids remain high.

"If the weather is very good," Michel Lafarge said, "I want to pick as late as possible. If the weather is bad, I feel I should pick as soon as possible."

For the *vigneron,* then, the challenge is to choose that right moment—not too soon, not too late. It is his yearly gamble with nature. But nature, as always, remains the great arbiter.

13

VENDANGE

Nature was kind in July and August of 1984. But the warm, dry, sunny days that *vignerons* pray for in September were few. I returned to Burgundy after a two-month absence on September 17, and from then through harvest, my diary is filled with dire reports:

"18 September—Cold, chilly. Rained all night."

"22 September—Cold, rainy."

"24 September—Chilly, damp, overcast."

"25 September—Unremitting rains."

The sun came out on the 27th and stayed through the next day. On October 1, there was heavy, ceaseless rain.

The grapes were not gaining much in sugar. Although the low temperatures were holding down the amount of rot that can develop with so much wetness, rot was nevertheless a problem on every *vigneron*'s mind. The *vendangeurs,* or pickers, for the Lafarges had arrived in Burgundy from many parts of France and from Belgium—students, a restaurateur and workers who save their vacation each year for the harvest.

On October 2, the sky was clear, and Michel Lafarge decided to begin his harvest. On this first day, the twenty pickers harvested in Le Village, the Volnay *Premier Cru* vineyard behind the Lafarge home, each person working down a row, cutting the clusters of Pinot Noir with a *sécateur,* a short, sharp-bladed clipper, and dropping them into a plastic basket. As the basket filled with about eight kilos (seventeen to eighteen pounds) of grapes, it was passed, bucket brigade fashion, to a *porteur,* who emptied it into his *caisse,* a rectangular container. With five or six basket-loads in it, the *caisse* weighed about one hundred pounds. The *porteur* then hefted it onto his shoulder and carried it to the winery. By late afternoon, with nearly all the vines clipped clean of their healthy clusters, the *vendangeurs* began clipping off the *deuxième génération,* second-growth clusters, which begin later than the normal clusters and remain small and green and hard, never really ripening. These, however, did not go into their baskets; they went at each other. Gérard threw grapes at Maryse. She threw grapes at Philippe. Daniel bounced a cluster off Valérie's shoulder. Bibi hurled a handful at Frédéric. The day's games had started. But suddenly they stopped, almost, one might say, in midair. Michel Lafarge had returned. "They do not throw grapes when I'm here," he said.

The next day, there would be no games. All through the night, in my room under the eaves where the window was on a slant over my bed, I could hear the rain. The room was very cold. By seven-thirty on the morning of October 3, in boots, pants and hooded rain jacket, I joined the other pickers in Michel Lafarge's *Premier Cru* Beaune-Grèves vineyards. The rain never stopped. The earth on the vineyard slope was slippery mud.

We clipped, filled our baskets and passed them to the *porteurs* —to Pierre, who was called Papy because he was the oldest of the young pickers; to Gérard, who was nicknamed Gégé, and to Jean Paul. In the Volnay Le Village vineyard, they had only to walk into the winery; here, they carried one hundred pounds on their shoulders about three hundred feet to the tractor, which could not get down the narrow, mud-gutted path to the vineyard.

Whenever I stood up to stretch, I could see other harvesters in the distance, hunched over other dripping vines, each *vigneron* with his own group of *vendangeurs* picking his own small patch of Beaune-Grèves. I also saw Michel Lafarge looking at a cluster of grapes in his hand and then up at the sky. He was not smiling.

At 9 A.M., there was a *casse-croûte,* a snack of cheese and ham, bread, fruit and hot chocolate. Then, back to the vineyard.

The rain continued. The temperature early that morning had been 39 degrees Fahrenheit. None of us was wearing gloves. By late morning, the cold had so permeated my hands that holding the *sécateur,* clipping, even dropping clusters into the basket, became difficult. Water ran down my sleeve. My pants were soaked. Maryse, who was working in the row next to mine, stood up to stretch. "Last year at this time, we were wearing shorts and T-shirts, and we were still hot," she said. The rain dripped down her face, and she crouched over again, checking her vines for every good cluster of grapes. Noon seemed a long time coming.

We drove back to Volnay, to lunch in the house of Michel Lafarge's parents, which had been opened, as it is every fall, for the harvest. The tractor followed slowly, hauling the *caisses* of grapes to the winery, to be put immediately into the stemmer-crusher and then in the fermenter.

Madame Nicolas, the cook for the pickers, had prepared a lunch of fresh vegetables, pâté, *blanquette de veau,* potatoes, cheese and fruit.

By 2 P.M., it was back to the vineyards for the harvesters, this time Volnay *Premier Cru* Clos des Chênes until 6 P.M., with a midafternoon break for wine.

The people who pick for Michel Lafarge are paid by the hour, not by the amount they pick: 24 francs (about $3) for *vendangeurs,* 25 francs (about $3.13) for *porteurs.* How much a harvester can pick in a day depends on the year and the conditions. "In 1982, a large harvest, the fastest picker harvested 350 kilos [770 pounds] a day," Michel Lafarge said. "In 1983, they averaged less than 100 kilos." In 1984, the average was 150 kilos.

The rain and cold continued into the next day. The harvesters finished Volnay Clos des Chênes and began the Volnay village appellation vineyards. They continued there through intermittent rain on Friday and Saturday. On Sunday, it was sunny, windy and chilly. The pickers finished in Volnay and moved on to the Bourgogne rouge appellation vineyards.

Monday, October 8, was cold and raw. The Lafarge harvesters completed Bourgogne rouge in the morning and began Meursault in the afternoon. Tuesday, October 9, was a cold, dark day. They finished in Meursault, and in the afternoon, started picking Bourgogne Aligoté.

On Wednesday, the sun shone through for a while; Bourgogne Aligoté was completed by lunchtime. Bourgogne Passetoutgrains was begun in the afternoon. The pickers continued there all of Thursday. By noon on Friday, the twelfth of October, they finished Passetoutgrains and, with it, the last of the Lafarge vineyards.

It was a gentle, sunny day, the kind of day every *vigneron* in Burgundy had hoped would come in September. As the *vendangeurs* prepared to leave the last vineyard of the harvest, they picked wildflowers to decorate the tractor and began the slow ride back to the winery, lights on at midday, horn blowing, pickers singing. Standing on the stone wall at the Place de l'Église, I could hear them before I spotted them. As they turned onto Route d'Autun, still a distance away, I saw them waving. A left turn up the road to the village, all noise and lights. They drove through Place de l'Église, cheering, turned left onto Rue de la Combe and up to the Lafarge winery. Neighbors came out to join the celebration. Noëlle Lafarge, who had been in the kitchen of the old house, setting the table for lunch, looked out of the ground-floor window and was presented with a bouquet of wildflowers plucked from the vineyard to decorate the tractor and now plucked from the tractor to present to the *vigneron*'s wife. Bibi and Papy guzzled wine. Richard ran to the second floor of the house to pour water on them. The group broke into a *ban bourguignon,* the Burgundian salute—singing "La, la, la, la, la, la, la, la, la, la, la," with arms raised, hands twisting right, then left, with every "la."

It was time to empty the *caisses* into the stemmer-crusher. Normally, it is the *porteurs'* task, but on the last day of the harvest, tradition calls for the young women to do it. "O.K.," the men shouted. "Heave ho, that's how. Heave ho. That's how."

Standing slightly to the side of the celebrating crowd, Michel Lafarge looked up at the sky. It was a perfect day, with soft, sensuous clouds floating lazily by. He spoke, almost to himself. "Think what a harvest it would have been if the weather had been like this all month."

That evening, there was the *Paulée,* the grand celebration that always follows the end of the harvest. I arrived early to help set the table for forty in a room that would comfortably seat twenty, be a bit crowded with twenty-five, be filled to bursting with thirty. But we were forty, and we pushed and jammed in forty places. We put wildflowers on each table. Madame Guigue, an elderly woman who had been the harvesters' cook for ten years,

Papy and Richard during the Lafarge harvest in Beaune-Grèves.

arrived and was given a great, noisy *ban bourguignon*. Michel Lafarge sat across from me, and as we all raised our arms to twist our hands at every "la," I could see his powerful hands stained red with new wine.

Jean Paul Colas, who works for Michel Lafarge throughout the year, arrived with his wife and two young sons. Gégé raised a toast to Michel with a glass of white wine and homemade *crème de cassis.*

Michel, looking very serious while his blue eyes were looking very mischievous, announced, "Perhaps next year I will buy a mechanical harvesting machine."

"What? No! Then we won't have a *Paulée.*"

"Even with a harvesting machine, we can have a *Paulée.*" Michel laughed.

We ate *quenelle* with *champignons* and white cream sauce, *poulet de Bresse, haricots verts,* salad. There was a platter of cheeses. There was *mousse au chocolat* with cream. We drank Meursault 1982, Bourgogne 1982 and Volnay Clos des Chènes 1981, with its lovely berry aroma.

And then we were given a mystery wine. "Guess the wine." Volnay by its aroma. Clos des Chènes by its fineness, its elegance. But as far as I pushed the vintage, I was years wrong. "Nineteen fifty-nine," Michel announced.

"Merci, Monsieur le Maire!" we all shouted, and gave him a *ban bourguignon.*

"Nicole, *une chanson,*" the *vendangeurs* shouted. "Nicole, *une chanson.*" And Nicole sang.

"Claude, *une chanson.* Claude, *une chanson.*"

"No, no, I cannot, I cannot."

"Who can sing? You? You? Maryse, *une chanson.* Maryse, *une chanson!*" Maryse obliged with a wonderful, throaty voice.

"Gérard, Pascal, Daniel, Valérie, *une chanson, une chanson.*"

And then, "Amérique, *une chanson;* Amérique, *une chanson.*"

The chant continued until "Amérique" sang—of sorts—squeaking and scratching away at "When the Saints Go Marching In." Luckily, the French knew it, and soon La France joined Amérique with a rousing "When zee zaints go marshin een . . . Oh, when zose zaints go marshin een . . . "

It was now 2 A.M. The *vendangeurs* had been in the vineyards

The harvest is over, and the *vendangeurs* cheer the vintner's wife.

at seven-thirty that morning. Some of them would be leaving the next day for Alsace, farther north, where the harvest was about to begin. Others would return to school and their jobs. But for the moment, they were still in Burgundy and there was one more song to sing.

"Je suis fier d'être Bourguignon," they sang. "I am proud to be a Burgundian." Louder and louder, their voices carrying out of the jammed little room, down Rue de la Combe, through Volnay.

"I am proud to be a *Bourguignon.* I am proud to be a *Bourguignon.*"

The harvest of '84 was over.

The Lafarge *Paulée.*

14

WINEMAKING IN VOLNAY

After the harvest, the leaves of the shorn vines—now russet and red and gold—fall. Within the bare, gnarled vine, the energy that is left goes to the roots, to be stored for next year. The sap no longer flows. The vine is dormant until the first warmth of spring awakens it and its life begins again.

As peace settles into the vineyards, the activity moves to the winery. In September, as the grapes were reaching their final ripening stage, the winery prepared for the harvest. Equipment was examined and cleaned; barrels were checked and put into place; everything that would be needed for the new grapes and the new wine was readied.

Michel Lafarge buys an average of twenty-five new barrels each year so that he has about two hundred barrels at all times. He buys them from the cooper Jacques Damy, and he orders them made with little toast.

During harvest, the grapes arrive at the winery twice a day —at midday and at the end of the workday. White grapes are pressed immediately, and the fresh juice is run off to be fermented. The Chardonnay of Meursault is put into small oak casks for its fermentation. The juice of Aligoté is fermented in large vats. After fermentation has been completed, both white wines are put into casks for aging, although Chardonnay remains in these small oak barrels about twice as long as Aligoté does.

When red grapes arrive, they are put into the stemmer-crusher, which removes the grapes from the stems and at the same time crushes the grapes very lightly. The process of stem-

Newly harvested grapes are dumped into the stemmer-crusher.

ming grapes is called *égrappage,* and it is not always used for Pinot Noir in Burgundy.

"For me, it depends on the year," Michel Lafarge said. "If the grapes are healthy and pretty, if there is no rot, I use some of the stems, though never more than 50 percent of them. But the stems must be green, not dry. If the stems are good, they add acidity, astringency. When the vintage is not so good, I stem completely. By not using stems in a bad year, we eliminate some of the rot." He has only to remove a screen within the equipment, and the grapes will not be stemmed.

With or without stems, as the year and Monsieur Lafarge dictate, the red grapes are crushed lightly and put with their skins —which contain color, tannin and other components—into the open-topped, glass-lined cement fermenters that are set along both sides of the ground-level winery.

"Fermentation must begin immediately," Monsieur Lafarge said as we stood near a wall of fermenters, each of which holds from 3,000 to 4,000 kilos of grapes. To assure that it will, he cuts a small quantity of grapes about a week before he expects to begin the harvest, and crushes them in a small container. As they warm up, the natural yeast on the skins begins to multiply.

"We call this starter *pied-de-cuve.* Some Burgundians buy ready-made yeast. I've always made mine. With this *pied-de-cuve,* we have an active starter ready before the harvest begins."

In fermentation, the yeast acts on the sugar in the grape juice, converting it to about half alcohol, half carbon dioxide, which escapes. In the early stages of fermentation, when the wine bubbles and froths and the temperature rises, the carbon dioxide pushes the skins, seeds and other solids fermenting with the red wine to the top, forming a cap, or *chapeau,* as the French call it. This cap is thick, often accounting for as much as a third of the depth of the fermenting juice, and it is crusty. All the color of a grape is in the skin, and the tannin comes from the skin and stems and seeds. To extract the color and tannin and other desirable components, the cap must be broken and pushed down into the fermenting juice. This can be done in a number of ways.

In many wineries, a hose is attached to the bottom of the fermenter and brought to the top. The valve is opened and with the help of a pump, fermenting juice from the bottom of the tank is pumped through the hose and sprayed over the cap, breaking it and pushing it down. This method is called pumping over.

In wineries that use shallow fermenters, a plunger not unlike a plumber's plunger with a long handle is used to push down the cap. The most modern—and expensive—method of breaking the cap is to use round, horizontal stainless-steel fermenting tanks. Whenever the winemaker wants to pump over, he simply pushes the correct button and the tanks rotate, breaking the cap and blending it with the fermenting juice.

Burgundy has always had its own system of breaking the cap. It is called the *pigeage,* and it requires no mechanism, no electricity, no equipment. It uses human bodies instead, strong young men who in past days wore nothing and now wear shorts to do the job. They climb to the top of the open fermenters, which at the Lafarge winery are nearly twelve feet high, and ease their way over the side. Holding on to a board across the top, they lower themselves into the vat, onto the cap, and slowly, by treading with their feet, break it. They then push down farther until they are thigh high in wine, kneading it with their feet and legs.

Ideally, the cap should be broken twice a day during fermentation. At Lafarge, it is done by pumping over in the morning, and by the *pigeage* each evening. One evening, at dusk, we watched from below as Papy, Bibi and Richard were doing the *pigeage.*

"We are very happy up here," Bibi shouted.

"It is so warm. Wine is always warm when it ferments," Papy called to us.

For about ten minutes, they worked the cap with their feet and legs. Then they climbed out and down and hosed off the wine and bits of grapeskin and seeds that clung to them.

When they had finished, the entire winery was washed down, as it is twice each day during harvest and fermentation. Cleanliness is one of the basic rules of good winemaking.

After eight to ten days, when all the sugar in the juice has been converted into alcohol and carbon dioxide, fermentation stops. The new wine is drawn off and put into *pièces,* Burgundian oak barrels. The solids—skins, seeds, sometimes stems, and other matter—are shoveled into the press. The first run of this press

The *pigeage* at the Lafarge winery.

wine is used with the new wine. The rest of the press wine i
separate for two to three months. If at the end of that
Monsieur Lafarge feels it is good enough, he uses it. If he feels
it is not up to the quality of its appellation, he may add it to one
of the lesser appellation wines.

Michel Lafarge usually leaves his Pinot Noir wines in barrel
for eighteen months, his Meursault for about twelve months, and
his Aligoté, Bourgogne and Passetoutgrains for less time, usually
about six to seven months. All barrel aging times may vary
slightly, depending on the year.

During a wine's time in barrel, solids settle to the bottom. To
clear the wine of this sediment, Michel Lafarge racks two or three
times. In racking, the wine is drawn out of the barrel, until just
before it becomes cloudy. The remaining wine, mixed with the
sediment on the bottom of the barrel, stays behind while the
clear, racked wine is put into a clean barrel. The first racking
takes place after the malolactic fermentation. In this secondary
fermentation, malic acid, which is harsh, is converted by certain
bacteria to lactic acid, which is softer, and to carbon dioxide. This
is not an alcohol fermentation and thus it does not result in an
addition or reduction of alcohol in the wine. A malolactic fermentation is especially important in cooler wine regions, where
the acidity is usually higher at the time of harvest than it generally is in more benign climates. Acid is necessary for a wine.
Though too little makes a wine dull and flabby, and too much
makes it overly tart, a balanced amount of acid will help a wine
to live longer and keep it tasting fresh and alive and interesting.

A malolactic fermentation is not likely to begin in bone-
chilling temperatures, and Burgundy's cellars are often heated to
encourage its start. Still, it may begin in autumn, it may begin in
spring, or it may begin in autumn, stop, and start again in spring.
Though in some wine regions of the world it must be artificially
induced by an inoculation of bacteria, the malolactic happens
naturally in Burgundy.

Before a wine is bottled, it is fined, which is a method of
clarifying it and removing any protein solids that may still be
floating in it. Michel Lafarge uses the traditional method of fining
for his red wine. For each barrel of wine, he takes the whites of
three or four fresh eggs, beats them in a bowl with a pinch of salt,

which helps the egg whites combine more readily with protein and other particles, and then adds the blend to the top of the barrel, mixing it into the wine with a *dodine*. This special tool has a long handle and a round metal plate dotted with holes, which is attached at a right angle to the handle. Slowly, very slowly, over about two months, the egg white mixture sinks, taking any protein afloat in the wine to the bottom of the barrel.

Monsieur Lafarge may do his second racking after fining and just before bottling, "but there is no rule about when this racking is done. The time depends on the wine."

Michel Lafarge may rack a third time. He may not. He may filter the wine before it is bottled. He may not. "Again, it depends on the quality of the year and the wine. If the wine is brilliant after fining, it is not necessary to filter it."

Eighteen to twenty months after the grapes are harvested, his Pinot Noir is put into the traditional slope-shouldered green Burgundy bottle and stored in deep, cool cellars through the heat of late spring and summer. In autumn, when the weather is temperate, he releases his wines. He sends them to other parts of France, to Switzerland, Belgium and Austria. And through Cannan & Wasserman, he sends them beyond the Continent, to Great Britain, the United States, to importers anywhere in the world to whom Becky Wasserman and Christopher Cannan sell wine.

15

CHANGES

Le Serbet moved from Beaune to Bouilland in 1982, settling into an office that had been fashioned out of the center of the farm's middle building. Centuries before, at the height of the farm's fortunes, it had been the home of the farmer and his family; and even though a part of its core was reworked, most of the building —with its old wood doors, its remnants of fireplaces and its rivulets of dried wallpaper streaming down its walls—remained a chipped mirror reflecting earlier times.

In its heart now were two pristine white offices, one flight up. A half flight below was a room that doubled as a kitchen for staff lunches and as a tasting room for clients. A flight above the office, under the rafters, a room and a bath were added. Becky now both lived and worked in Bouilland.

During the next year, as the business expanded, Becky began to look for a *stagiaire,* a trainee who was bright enough to do office chores, mature enough to accompany guests on visits to domaines and, at the same time, willing to do everything else that needed to be done—meet visitors at the railroad station, keep the wine cellar in order, run errands and feed Thatcher, the cat. He had to drive a car, speak French and English, know or want to know about Burgundy's wines, pick up samples from vintners, pack boxes, haul them to the post office and, like all *stagiaires* in all French businesses, do it all for low wages and long hours and on the bottom rung of the staff ladder.

Becky was flooded with applications for the job. While she was pondering the choice, she received a call from David Patterson, an American friend who lived in London. He knew a young man who wanted to do a *stage* in the wine trade in France. He was English, spoke some French, drove a car, had worked in wineries, knew wine and was very reliable. "How old is he?" Becky asked.

"Twenty-three or twenty-four, I believe, and quite mature," Mr. Patterson answered.

On New Year's Eve, just as 1984 was about to arrive, Becky drove to the Beaune railroad station to meet her new English *stagiaire.* As passengers came off the train, she looked for a blond young man about six feet tall. The platform cleared until there was one blond young man about six feet tall and there was Becky.

"Bertie Eden?" she asked.

"Mrs. Wasserman?" he asked.

"How old are you?"

"Nineteen."

Bertie Eden spoke almost no French, but he learned fast. He knew nothing about Burgundy's wine, but he learned fast. He drove a car—and he drove fast.

Soon after Bertie joined Le Serbet, Jean Pierre and Isabelle Silva, the young couple who owned Vieux Moulin, the restaurant down the road from the farm, asked Becky if she would like a puppy. Their beautiful amber-eyed, reddish-blond dog had had a visitor one night and now they had eight little ones, none of whom looked like their mother. And so black-and-brown Sydney, who had been weaned from mother's milk to Vieux Moulin cuisine and did not take easily to canned dog food, joined Le Serbet. His care and feeding and training were added to Bertie's list of duties.

At nineteen, Bertie was still little more than a pup himself, but he had packed those years full. Born in London in 1964, the son of Lord Eden of Winton and a grandnephew of Anthony Eden, Robert Frederick Calvert Eden lived first with his mother after his parents were divorced and later with his father. When he was seventeen, he decided to go to Australia.

"My father gave me a round-trip ticket and said, 'If you earn your own way so that you bring back the return half, I'll double its inflationary value.' I did; I brought it back."

In Australia, Bertie traveled mostly by hitchhiking and jumping on and off freight trains. And he managed, usually on a dollar a day, by doing odd jobs along the way. For two weeks and two hundred dollars he picked avocados. "I lived in a barn that had a roof but no walls." For two months he worked in a coal mine. "Rather than dig out coal by hand, we used a machine, a crane called a walking dragline. I lived in the coal mining camp with some pretty rough people. We worked seven days a week."

Bertie also worked at two Australian wineries, pruning vines, harvesting grapes and doing cellar chores.

A year passed quickly, and when February came he left for Italy, where he worked for a while at Castelli dei Rampolla in Tuscany, a winery owned by the di Napoli family.

His next spell of experience came in Sardinia, at the Hotel Forte Village, where he served wine and wiped silver and had no days off.

After three months in Sardinia, he returned to England to have a talk with his father. "How do you propose I carry on?" he asked. "I want to go into the wine trade and I want to go to California."

"I think I'm very fortunate," Bertie later told me. "My father was in politics for thirty years—he was minister of industry during Edward Heath's regime. He has never been the type to tell me what to do; instead, he's always encouraged me to do what I wanted."

When Bertie found he couldn't get a permit to work in the United States, his father asked a friend, David Patterson, if he could help Bertie get a job in the wine trade in France. Mr. Patterson, who knew Becky, called her, and Bertie Eden became Le Serbet's *stagiaire*.

I met Bertie soon after he had arrived at Le Serbet, when I returned to the farm in Bouilland, renting the room under the eaves, above Le Serbet's offices. During the day, light streamed in through the skylight on the slant just above the bed. On a clear night, lying in bed, I could look up and see six of the seven stars of the Big Dipper.

One evening as we sat around the fireplace in the house, I asked Bertie what he did at Le Serbet.

"I assist Becky and Dominique. I'm being trained to take clients around to suppliers. I put through orders and send telexes —you know, like any ordinary office boy. But most of all, I work directly for Becky and do whatever she asks me to do, and I'm quite happy to do so."

When he arrived, Becky had said to her young *stagiaire,* "Bertie, you're now in the wine trade, whether you like it or not."

Bertie had grinned. "That's why I'm here—to train for the wine trade."

"All right," Becky said. "Your first assignment . . ."

"Yes?" asked Bertie, all eagerness.

". . . is to call in the sheep."

"The sheep?"

"This is a wine brokerage, but it's also a working farm."

Becky still remembers Bertie marching across the sheep pastures, roaring, *"Viens, donc. Viens. Viens!"*

Five days a week, it is Paul Gutigny, not Bertie, who takes care of the farm's needs. A tall, sinewy man, patient and bashful, Paul Gutigny has worked for Becky since 1975. Born in Burgundy about twenty miles from Bouilland, Monsieur Gutigny grew to be a strong lad, and when he was a young teen-ager, he began to work in the fields. "My family did not own a farm. We had only three cows and four sheep. We worked for other people."

After he married Christiane in 1956, he rented a farm, but it proved too small to support his family, which soon included two sons. In 1964, he bought a farm up in the hills above the valley of Bouilland. "I had saved very hard, but I had only about half the amount. I paid that and I paid the *notaire,* and borrowed the rest from the bank. Christiane and I worked hard. It was tough, so tough. And yet we never had enough money. One day I called the real estate agent and said, 'I want to sell the farm for 350,000 francs.' The agent came right over to the farm and looked around. 'But why do you want to sell? Do you have debts? Do you owe the butcher? The baker? What?'

"I told him, No, I have no debts; it is the bank. The bank wanted its money, too much, too fast. It gave us only eight years

Paul Gutigny.

to pay for the farm, and no matter how hard we worked, we could not make it. The agent sold the farm for 380,000 francs. After we paid him, the bank and the *notaire*, we had 170,000 francs, just what we started with. In six years of hard work, we had not made one franc."

Becky met Christiane when their children were students at Bouilland's one-room schoolhouse, and soon after that, Paul came to work at Becky's farm. Christiane, too, has worked for Becky periodically.

"He does everything," Becky said of Paul. "He takes care of the large vegetable and flower gardens. He takes care of the animals. He butchers eight or ten lambs a year for us. We sell the rest. He takes care of the chickens, the geese, the goats, the rabbits. He does the masonry. He's also an A-one taster—very decisive about what he likes and why."

Paul Gutigny also cuts the wood for the fireplace. Bouilland lives on its dairy products and its wood; and wood was the major product long before cows. "In the nineteenth century," Monsieur Gutigny said, "Bouilland had about thirty families, and at least twenty-five of them lived by selling wood."

The village of Bouilland, tiny in itself, owns eight hundred hectares (almost two thousand acres) of forest. "Mostly oak, birch and beech," Paul Gutigny said, "and the forests are so big that in one's whole lifetime of cutting trees, it is very rare that you would cut in the same place twice."

Each taxpaying resident of the village pays 120 francs to the village for the right to cut an area of about forty by fifty meters (approximately 44 by 55 yards) a year. "That comes to about thirty cubic meters of wood," Paul Gutigny added. "A man can sell just one big tree for about three times the price of the permit."

Monsieur Gutigny, who is called Grand Paul when Becky's son Petit Paul is at the farm, cuts the wood in December, a job that takes about ten days. He stacks it in the forests until June, when the forest and the wood have dried after winter, and he hauls it back to the farm.

"It's almost enough for the season," Becky says, "although it wouldn't be if we used the fireplace every evening. In winter, when Bouilland turns icy damp, we spend more time in the dining room. That room is much smaller, the ceiling is much lower, and it has a wood-burning stove that uses less wood."

In 1978, Becky's mother died. She was buried in Bouilland, in the graveyard of the village church. A beautiful woman, she had always dressed impeccably and well. At the time of her death, Becky was "in my jeans period," she says. At the funeral, however, she wore a black skirt, black top, black hat, gloves and her mother's mink jacket. "I looked in the mirror and wasn't sure I liked what I saw, but everyone at the funeral said to me, 'That's the way Granny would have liked you to dress today.' "

"Granny had *l'intelligence de coeur,*" Pamela de Villaine said. "She had no pretense. She left warm memories with everyone who knew her."

As Becky's brokerage grew, her need to be at the source of her work was undeniable. Bart Wasserman, however, needed to be where his work received daily sustenance, and Burgundy was not that place. Finally, from the world they had made together, one had to stay and one had to leave. Becky and Bart separated.

16

VISITORS TO THE FARM

With endings came beginnings. The staff of Le Serbet was solid now. Becky, Dominique and Bertie worked well together. In the year between completing school and leaving for a trip to Australia, Paul Wasserman, bilingual and mature beyond his teen years, joined the staff. There was humor in the office, and there was flexibility; and at Le Serbet, where no one day is like another, humor and flexibility matter very much.

The telex clicks; the telephone calls come in from America, Australia, England; guests arrive from at least as many places. Or it may be a day when the loudest noise is Sydney's snores coming from his favorite office chair. The staff must rise with the tide and go with the flow.

"Le Serbet has no formal contracts with its suppliers," Becky said. "Just moral ones, which means we must be the best. We must have the importers, the markets. We must offer people who come to taste and buy our wines good visits and good hospitality."

Hospitality comes easily to Becky. When she was the wife of an artist, the house in Saint-Romain and then the farm were always crossroads for visitors to Burgundy. Now, as a wine and barrel broker, as head of Le Serbet, as an entrepreneur, Becky welcomes clients and both old and new friends, and rarely a week goes by without a guest.

Jon Winroth, who first came with Steven Spurrier in 1973,

Dominique Lafon and Bertie Eden in the courtyard of the farm.

arrived one May day from Paris with a kilo of Ethiopian coffee beans and a crusty, hand-shaped bread made by the Parisian baker Max Poilâne. We drank to his arrival with Michel Lafarge's Aligoté 1981, made from very old vines and wonderfully rich and full. Later, Jon, Becky, Bertie and I gathered around the fireplace for dinner—pilaf with lamb and pignolia nuts, spiced with curry, tarragon and thyme, and downed not with Burgundy this time but with André Roux's Château du Trignon 1982 from the Côtes du Rhône.

Jon's wife, Doreen, arrived the next day, and Bertie declared he would cook dinner. *Poulet à l'estragon* served with a sauce deglazed with vinegar, and with Jon's wonderful Paris bread. What wine would go with Bertie's feast? A bottle found in the back of the wine cellar, dusty and crusted and unlabeled.

"What is it?"

"Can't be sure."

"Maybe a Chablis."

It was opened and poured, a rich golden liquid.

We sniffed.

"Possibly a *Grand Cru* Chablis."

"Possibly from the sixties?"

We tasted.

"Oh, my," Becky said.

"Oh, my," I said.

"Oh, my, oh, my," Doreen Winroth said.

"Mmmmmmm," Bertie said.

Jon just smiled.

One chilly day, Jerry Goldstein of Acacia Winery in Napa Valley, which buys barrels through Le Serbet, drove up in a sleek gray car.

"Hello, hello, how's everybody?" he called in a voice that sounded like an overloaded old car rumbling up a dirt road.

An apéritif at the farm; then lunch at Vieux Moulin before starting an afternoon of tasting at Pousse d'Or and Domaine Lafon.

On a September evening, Michael Broadbent, who is head of the wine department of Christie's in London, and his wife, Daphne, came to dinner. The lamb was fresh and delicious. The Richebourg 1966 was mature and memorable.

The wines of Provence were the highlight when Leslee Reis, owner and chef of Café Provençal in Chicago, visited with her husband, Andy. Domaine des Planes Blanc de Blancs Muscat and Côte de Provence 1983; and a Saint André de Figuière 1982.

David Lett and his son Jason came to Bouilland in early spring. David, the winemaker and owner of The Eyrie Vineyards in Oregon, was the first person to plant Pinot Noir in that northwestern state, beginning in 1966. Fourteen years later, Robert Drouhin, the Burgundian *négociant,* organized a blind tasting, in France, of wines made of Pinot Noir. Much to every Frenchman's surprise—not least of all Drouhin's—The Eyrie Vineyard's 1975 Pinot Noir came in second, a scant 0.2 of a point behind Drouhin's 1959 Chambolle-Musigny, putting Oregon and Eyrie and Lett on the oenological map.

David came to Burgundy to learn more about Pinot Noir and Chardonnay. Teen-aged Jason came to learn more about ruins—of abbeys and chapels and all stones that whispered medieval secrets. On a drizzly afternoon, the three of us hiked up the western slope of Bouilland to the village's first fame, the ruins of the Abbey of Saint Marguerite, whose silent, roofless walls date back over eight hundred years. From that height, the grazing fields and the dimpled valley of Bouilland are spread below, green and softly beautiful even under lead-shaded skies. That evening, we toasted our hike with an Alsace Pinot Gris 1976 at Vieux Moulin.

During the Letts' stay on the farm, Richard and Thekla Sanford of Sanford Winery in Buellton, California, came by for a visit. Bertie, lacking a sword for the grand gesture, beheaded a bottle of Lechère Champagne in one swift swoop with a kitchen knife. Here's to Bertie, we all cheered, toasting him with golden bubbles.

For several weeks, Dr. William Pannell and his wife, Sandra, a cheery couple from Australia who own a small vineyard there named Mosswood, breezed in and out. They spent their days visiting vintners, other hours at the farm—joining in to set and clear the table for our big communal meals, hauling in logs for the fireplace.

Importer Freddy Wildman and his wife, Adrianna, took Becky and me to lunch at Vieux Moulin one Friday in spring.

"Wine is as various as humanity is," Freddy said, full of good cheer and good talk. "How do you decide which grape is noble and which is ignoble? The grapes of Rioja are noble to me." We talked about the old days when Becky first met Freddy at Aubert and Pamela de Villaine's wedding. "Aubert is almost my brother. I've known him so long and so well," Freddy said. "He is one of the nicest, one of the finest gentlemen."

Dessert was upon us, a cart of beguiling temptations. "No," Freddy said. "I'm diabetic, you know." He took a second look. "Oh, well," he sighed, and removed a small syringe from his jacket pocket. He lifted his shirt, gave himself an insulin shot in the belly and ordered dessert.

There were clients from London and Texas and Saint Louis and Detroit. There was Bertie's brother-in-law Ron Brown and his friend Andrew Gammon, who played Becky's harpsichord beautifully. There was a young man in the English wine trade named Jonathan, who stayed for a day and a night and played the piano beautifully.

There was Robert Joseph, an old friend of Becky's and editor of the fast-growing English magazine *What Wine?,* who stayed at the farm while he wrote stories about the harvest.

And there were Pete and Florence Stern. Pete owns Connoisseur Wines, Ltd., a shop in Chicago that carries one of the largest collections of estate-bottled Burgundies in the country.

Unlike most retailers, who choose their wines from importers and distributors in the States, Pete Stern goes to the source twice a year to find his own Burgundies. "I've tasted Gevrey-Chambertin from six growers so far this week," he told me one evening at Becky's. "Tomorrow, I'll decide which one—or ones—I'll order."

Pete, Florence and I spent the next day visiting cellars. We tasted still other Gevrey-Chambertin—those of Alain Burguet. We tasted five Vosne-Romanée and a Nuits-Saint-Georges and an Échézeaux at Domaine Jacqueline Jayer, where young Étienne Grivot is winemaker. We stopped at Savigny-lès-Beaune to taste the wines of Capron-Manieux.

A tall, wiry man in his sixties, Pete Stern has filled one life with many careers and interests. Born in Chicago, he became a jazz fan when he was a teen-ager. And he loves to tell stories about Teddy Wilson, Roy Eldridge, Zutty Singleton and Fletcher Henderson; about how Zutty Singleton became one of his closest friends; and how Pete took Florence to New York to meet Zutty before they were married. "Zutty made red beans and rice, New Orleans style," Pete remembers. "His wedding gift to us was the recipe."

That was for fun. For a living, Pete was in advertising briefly, before joining his father in the clothing business. He ended that career in 1961, the year he and Florence were married, and they went to Europe for their honeymoon. It was his first trip to the Continent and, as it turned out, his first encounter with great wine.

"I still remember that first wine. We were in a restaurant in Paris; the waiter handed me the wine list and asked me what I'd like to order. Hell, I didn't know one from another. He suggested Musigny. I said fine. It was my first great wine, and it was spectacular. We stayed in Europe for five weeks, over two of them in France, and every night for two weeks, I would order Musigny. But it was never as good as it was the first night, and I wondered why.

"When I returned to Chicago, I asked a few friends what wines to buy, but I ended up with Bordeaux that no one told me I should lay down, so I drank them before they were ready.

"About a year later, Florence and I returned to France. I remember we were at the Hôtel de la Poste in Avallon one evening. I couldn't speak French then, and the sommelier couldn't speak English, but he suggested the Musigny of Comte de Vogüé. Terrific. Back in Chicago, I bought four cases of it, and boy, they were real good. I began to get a picture of the complexity of Burgundy."

In the years after his marriage to Florence, Pete was a stockbroker. His hobbies were sailboats and wine. Slowly, wine began to move past the hobby stage until it teetered on the brink of vocation. It was pushed past that edge when a stockbroker friend called Pete in the mid-seventies to say he was going into the wine business and would Pete be his paid consultant. "Well, that was great for my ego, but what it really did was give me the impetus to do something serious about wine myself.

"In November of 1976, I found a tiny place in a brownstone

and opened my first wineshop in it. At first, the landlord wouldn't even let me put a sign out. I bought some beautiful wines from Bob Haas, but after two, three years, I realized I had almost all Haas wines and felt I had to expand. Becky Wasserman visited me in 1980 and showed me her list. I told her, 'You know, you have people I never heard of. I can't buy them.' Later, I got a letter from Steven Spurrier suggesting I try some of Becky's wines. Becky visited me again. And this time I told her I can't buy without tasting. 'Then why don't you come to Burgundy to taste with me?' she said."

And that is what he did in June 1981. "I had moved to my present shop the year before and I had much more space and a cellar. I bought many wines from Becky on that trip. I still buy Burgundies from Bob Haas, and from other people I visit in Burgundy, but I continue to buy a great deal from Becky."

The day's work was over now, and Pete, Florence and I were tasting wine for the sheer pleasure of it—Domaine Roulot Meursault Les Luchets 1981 and a Nuits-Saint-Georges Les Chaignots 1982 of Alain Michelot. The mood was mellow. The food was marvelous. The restaurant? Vieux Moulin.

17

VIEUX MOULIN

Mist hung like a gauzy lace curtain that had been spread low over the valley of Bouilland during the night. Later it would rise, and if we were lucky, the sun would peer through. But as I walked down the road from the farm to the Hostellerie du Vieux Moulin at five forty-five, the mist still lay close to the ground, a sea of white, parting and swirling around me under a gossamer cover.

At Vieux Moulin, Jean Pierre Silva was waiting, tall and trim and smiling, and in the frail early-morning light, we drove off to the *marché* in Chalon-sur-Saône, an open food market some thirty miles south of Bouilland.

There are other *marchés* in Burgundy where twice a week Jean Pierre's father markets for the restaurant. But Chalon is the special one, the largest and the most beautiful of all the region's markets. And each Friday, the twenty-eight-year-old chef drives there to choose among fruits and vegetables, flowers, fresh herbs and little wild delicacies from the woods and fields of Burgundy, and from regions far from Burgundy.

The market spreads out across a large square a few hundred yards from the Saône River, the watery spine of Chalon. Dominating one end of the square is the Church of Saint Vincent, which had its beginning in the eleventh century. Hemming in the other three sides are buildings, some as old as the church, that house cafés and shops and wholesalers specializing in pâtés, bananas, horse meat, poultry, seafood and coffee. Soon after dawn, the market begins to stir. Wholesalers open their doors. Vendors in the square arrange foods and flowers in their stalls. Oranges and tomatoes are built into pyramids. Flowers are tied into bouquets.

In the long, narrow shop of a produce wholesaler, Jean Pierre starts his work. He chooses plump, tender mushrooms—called *boutons de guêtre,* he says, "because they resemble the little buttons found on women's shoes in the nineteenth century." He chooses succulent strawberries, their rich perfume overpowering the aroma of all other fruits near them. Valencia oranges and sunny lemons, both from Spain. Young, pale-green zucchini. White asparagus. Great rosy tomatoes. Bright young carrots. Leeks. A sack of potatoes.

The market is humming now. The fresh foods gleam with colors so clear and pure, and textures so firm and sumptuous, they are like small sculptures. The noise swells. Vendors greet Jean Pierre. *"Bonjour, bonjour, Monsieur Silva."* "Ah, Jean Pierre," Madame Lafond calls from behind her fortress of flowers, her cheeks glowing as pink as her posies. *"Bonjour, ça va?"*

"Oui, ça va. Et vous?" he answers, nimbly feeling the flowers' stems. He buys a garden's worth, from Madame Lafond and from other flower vendors: blossoms still furled like umbrellas, which will open in the dining room of Vieux Moulin.

With his dark, lively eyes, he surveys the sea of stalls, homing in on the best. He buys wild asparagus, that exotic little vegetable that resembles tiny green shafts of wheat; garlic on pale-green stalks; bunches of chervil so fresh and dewy one could fashion them into a bouquet and tuck it in a vase. He buys oak leaf, the red-tinged salad green. He buys tiny carrots, fresh fennel, fresh dill, rhubarb, turnips, and artichokes that look like enormous green roses. The aromas grow. The crowds grow. The noise grows. The colors swirl together. The air is sweet and tart and tangy—and cold.

Jean Pierre deposits our armloads on a wheelbarrow near the produce wholesaler and by eight-fifteen, our fruit and vegetable and flower marketing finished, he points. "The café over there, Le Saint Vincent." We nudge through the *marché* and edge around stalls to a half-timbered building that leans out, like an aged coquette beckoning. Inside, it is welcomingly warm. The coffee steams. The croissants are flaky.

Jean Pierre Silva wheels away his purchases at the market in Chalon-sur-Saône.

As we sip our coffee, friends come over to greet Jean Pierre. They shake hands, pull up chairs and order more coffee, more croissants. They are Burgundian restaurateurs who, like Jean Pierre, do their marketing in Chalon. Jean Luc Dauphin. Monique Parra. Jacques Laine. Madame Pianetti-Voarick. Restaurateurs from Beaune, from Nuits-Saint-Georges, from villages only slightly larger than Bouilland.

As we leave, still another friend enters, damp cigarette clamped between his lips. "Jean Pierre, why are you leaving?"

"*Au revoir.* Until next Friday," he calls back. We skirt around the sides of the square, past wholesalers, fat bananas, bloodied hares and quail, skating across bits of vegetable leaves, fruit and broken flowers that twig brooms will later sweep away. Lured to the heady aromas of the coffee shop, Jean Pierre buys three kinds —Brazilian, mocha and a blend for breakfast.

Then he rolls the wheelbarrow down the side street to his van, loads it and heads back to Bouilland. Friday morning's work is done.

On other days, in other places, Jean Pierre buys other foods. Poultry and eggs and rabbits from local farms. Lamb and Charolais beef from René Bize, the butcher in Savigny-lès-Beaune. Baby pigeons from Monsieur Megrot in Cussigny, about twelve miles from Bouilland. Tiny *fromages de chèvre* from Madame L'Huillier in Bouilland.

Across the road from the restaurant, the senior Monsieur Silva has set out a vegetable garden, which he tends. Behind the restaurant is an herb garden. The cherries that grow on the tree near the entrance to the restaurant and which are too sour to eat are made into vinegar. And fresh trout comes from the little Rhoin River, which flows through the *hostellerie*'s property, so close to the restaurant that it forms a boundary between one of the dining room's windowed walls and the stretch of lawn and trees beyond it.

From such beginnings, great things are created. Fresh herbs play an important part in Jean Pierre's cooking. So does vinegar. But they never overwhelm; they enhance. He works with a deft hand.

To prepare his *vinaigrette de pigeonneau aux petits légumes de saison* (squab in vinegar sauce with baby vegetables of the season), one of my favorite Vieux Moulin dishes, he browns the legs and filets of the young pigeon, leaving the inside rosy, cuts the filet into thin slices and arranges the slices and the legs on the plate like an open fan, closing the fan at one end with baby vegetables, which might include zucchini, wild asparagus, carrots, yellow squash and pearl onions, among others, and spoons over the arrangement a tangy sauce made of pigeon stock, Sherry vinegar and walnut oil.

His *terrine gourmande aux racines, petite salade à l'huile de noisette* brings together in a terrine chopped veal, sweetbreads, *foie gras,* carrots, asparagus and turnips with the rich flavoring of truffle juice, Port, nutmeg and chives, and arrives at the table dressed with a salad of tiny potatoes, radishes and beets seasoned with walnut oil and Sherry vinegar.

In Jean Pierre's presentation of *pintade,* the guinea fowl, quartered and browned in butter, is served in a sauce based on an intensely rich *pintade* stock, heavy cream, tea, orange zest and honey, and is accompanied by wild rice.

In his presentation of *jambonette de grenouilles, estouffade de jeunes poireaux,* sautéed frogs' legs are served with young leeks and in a red wine sauce to which a *mirepoix,* a sautéed blend of carrots, shallots and parsley, has been added.

The dessert cart at Vieux Moulin makes strong wills weak. *Bavarois au chocolat. Bavarois aux fraises des bois. Meringue au chocolat. Oeufs à la neige* with *crème anglaise.* Pears cooked in red wine and spices. Cakes and tartes and sorbets and cloud-light, air-soft mousses. I've been with friends who, unable to decide, have had two and three. And I watched one intrepid young man order— and eat—five.

Just as Vieux Moulin's dishes come from the region's sources, the restaurant's wine list, too, has mined the region's riches. Most of the wines are, not surprisingly, from Burgundy, and all of them have been chosen by Jean Pierre and his wife, Isabelle.

"On Wednesday and on Thursday morning, when the restaurant is closed, and especially in winter, when we have more time, we visit *vignerons* to taste wines," Jean Pierre said. "We have close to four thousand bottles in the *caves* now. We buy only a little of each wine at a time and then, if it sells, we go back for more. After all, we're not far from the *vignerons.*"

In a short time, he and Isabelle have amassed a list that includes the finest and most representational selection of high-quality estate-bottled Burgundies I have found on any restaurant wine list—in Burgundy or elsewhere. Other restaurants may have longer lists; others have larger selections of older bottles. But none offers such abundant choice of good, sound—and affordable—wines. There are 310 wines on the list, and 260 are Burgundies. Of the 260, 175 are red, 83 are white and 2 are rosé.

The other fifty wines are from other wine regions of France. Fifty of the 310 are available in half bottles. There are also nearly two dozen Champagnes, an equal number of marc, the regional brandy distilled from grape pressing and highly prized among Burgundians, and ten choices among Port, Calvados and Armagnac.

But to return to the Burgundies.

While Romanée-Conti and La Tâche are represented by one vintage each, the *Premiers Crus* of Vosne-Romanée are represented by ten; Volnay, village appellation and *Premier Cru,* by eleven choices, which include Michel Lafarge's Volnay and Clos des Chènes; Meursault, village and *Premier Cru,* by ten; Pommard by ten; and various vineyards of Puligny-Montrachet and Chassagne-Montrachet by ten, plus nine of Le Montrachet and other *Grands Crus* of these two villages. Savigny-lès-Beaune, the nearest wine village and the largest seller in the restaurant, has sixteen choices on the list. There are also seven from Chambolle-Musigny, plus three Le Musigny.

The oldest wine on the list, in fact, is Le Musigny 1966 of Faiveley, followed by two 1969s—Le Corton (Bouchard Père et Fils) and Volnay Taillepieds (Hubert de Montille). Monsieur de Montille's 1972 Volnay Champans is also listed.

Jean Pierre Silva was born in Lyon, in the southernmost reaches of Burgundy, and began working in restaurants while he was still in his teens. It was at the restaurant La Mourrachonne on the Riviera, he says, that he really learned to cook.

"Guy Tricon and Jean Andres were the owners and chefs, and they were like second parents to me," he recalled. Along with another set of parents, Jean Pierre acquired a wife at La Mourrachonne. Isabelle worked in the dining room.

When La Mourrachonne closed, the young Silvas and the senior Silvas went to Isola, in the Alps, where they operated a ski resort. In 1981, the Hostellerie du Vieux Moulin was for sale, and the four Silvas bought it.

They came to tiny Bouilland—to the white picket fence that separates the *hostellerie* from the narrow road; to the two-story white building that houses the restaurant on the ground floor and the four Silvas plus the young Silvas' daughters, Laure and Doro-thée, on the second floor; to the property's other two-story build-ing, with its eight rooms for guests; and to the waterfall of the Rhoin River behind the *hostellerie,* which roars and swirls in roiling fury even though it is barely eight feet wide and falls, at most, a few yards.

Vieux Moulin means old mill, and once there was a mill here. Although the mill is gone, the millhouse still stands, the base of today's restaurant. It was reborn after World War II as a small bar and tobacco shop with a large open terrace. The proprietress was Madame Lebreuil, and because her patrons were often as hungry as they were thirsty, she began to serve *truite à la crème.* Nothing else. Just *truite à la crème.* The trout were plucked from the Rhoin River outside the back door, and the dish became the specialty of the little village. But Madame discovered—and it was difficult for her to believe—that some people who came to her little bar and wanted to eat did not want to eat *truite à la crème.* For those patrons, she finally agreed to have a little something else—pâté, beef, sausage. The seeds of a restaurant had been planted.

About twenty years ago, Madame Lebreuil sold her property to Raymond Heriot. His father, who Jean Pierre Silva tells me had a reputation as a fine chef, ruled the kitchen. Raymond ruled the dining room. The Heriots enclosed Madame Lebreuil's ter-race to make a spacious dining room. They also opened the eight bedrooms that turned the restaurant into a *hostellerie,* or inn.

After the elder Monsieur Heriot's death, Raymond cooked until 1981, when he sold Vieux Moulin to the Silva family.

Vieux Moulin's dining room looks out, on three sides, to trees and flowers, shrubbery and lawns. In the center of the dining room is a stone fountain surrounded by flowering plants. On the white-clothed tables, Jean Pierre's specialties are served on Villeroy & Boch china patterned in a pastel yellow, green and coral interplay of fruits and flowers. Despite the dining room's spaciousness, there are only a dozen tables, which accommodate, at most, sixty diners. To service them, there are three in attendance and Isabelle.

One sunny Saturday morning in June, Jean Pierre telephoned. "There is a young American here and I think he wants to work for me. But I am not sure. He does not speak French."

I walked down the road to Vieux Moulin and found the young American, who had parked his backpack against the outside wall.

"Boy, this is a tough place to find," he said.

"Why were you looking for it?"

"Because I heard about it from someone in the States. It sounds like a great restaurant, and Mr. Silva sounds like a great chef, and I kind a thought I might like to work here."

"Have you worked in a restaurant?"

"Yes, I'm working in one now, in Chicago."

"Which one?"

"Well, it's not exactly in Chicago. Near Chicago, in the suburbs."

"Ask him what kind of cuisine this restaurant near Chicago serves," Jean Pierre said to me.

"Tell him it specializes in the new California cuisine," the young American told me.

"What is this new California cuisine?"

"Explain it," I said to the young man.

"Tell him it's fresh fruits, fresh vegetables. A lot of baby vegetables. Herbs. It's using the foods of the region."

"That's new?" Jean Pierre asked.

"Tell him I'll work very hard. I'll work long hours. I'll do anything, just so I can learn from him."

"How long does he plan to stay?" Jean Pierre asked.

"A year, two years—whatever Mr. Silva wants."

Isabelle joined us. "What about insurance? He must carry insurance."

Jean Pierre Silva in the kitchen of Vieux Moulin.

"And he must buy his own white jackets for the kitchen," Jean Pierre added.

"I'll buy insurance. I'll buy white jackets."

"How much notice must you give your boss in, I mean, near Chicago?"

"It's O.K. I already told him I might not be back."

"When could he start?" Jean Pierre asked.

"Couple of days. Well, I really didn't think I'd get the job, so I told my brother I'd meet him in Paris for a few days."

"He'll report in two weeks," I told Jean Pierre.

"You'll report in two weeks," I told the young American.

"That's terrific. I think I'll head back to Paris now and maybe take some French lessons. I can't believe it. It was so easy."

I couldn't believe it either. "It was so easy," I said to Jean Pierre.

"Now it's easy. Wait until he's in the kitchen."

Two weeks later, the young American was in the kitchen. Four weeks later, he was out of it.

However hard the work at Moulin, it is done under the best conditions—a large, airy, immaculate kitchen with white walls and tiled floors. There, Jean Pierre rules in the traditional outfit of the French chef: pristine white cotton jacket, black-and-white herringbone cotton trousers, and clogs with leather tops, thick wooden soles and rubber bottoms.

One morning when I walked over to visit him in the kitchen, he was preparing a few of the day's desserts—*meringue au chocolat, bavarois aux fraises de bois* and *oeufs à la neige*—moving from one to the next.

Mixing chocolate with a rubber spatula in a large bowl. Placing it over a pot of simmering water on the stove. Beating cream into the chocolate. Coating a mold with butter and sugar. Purée-ing strawberries. Whipping *crème Chantilly.* Dissolving gelatin in water. Combining gelatin with strawberry *coulis* in a copper pot. Beating egg whites and sugar. Placing fluffy white dollops of it in a large oval pan of simmering water. Removing the airy puffs of egg white from the hot water, placing them on linen towels to drain and cool.

[132]

While Jean Pierre prepared desserts, a second cook cut up fowl. Another worker peeled oranges and divided them into sections that would decorate a dessert. Simmering on the stove were huge pots of vegetables and the carcasses of guinea fowl, to make the stock that would become the base of the zesty sauce of tea, orange peel and honey to serve with *pintade.* A basket of morels arrived. Jean Pierre checked them, and then checked on the other cooks and kitchen help. He turned to me. "It's quiet in the kitchen this morning."

Late one Thursday morning, Isabelle, Jean Pierre and I shared an apéritif in the reception room: a cherry wine made by Monsieur Joannet, who lives in Arcenant, about ten miles from Bouilland. Jean Pierre, who had been working in the herb garden when I arrived, was wearing a sweatshirt and jeans. Across the sweatshirt was a picture of Snoopy, sitting in front of a rainbow and saying:

> *Ne negligeons pas*
> *Le fait que je suis*
> *Peut-être génial.*

Neglect the fact that you are perhaps a genius? How could I, Jean Pierre?

As the fresh raw materials change with the season, so does Vieux Moulin's menu. Here, collected across seasonal lines, are four of Jean Pierre Silva's specialties. They have been tested in an American kitchen and adjusted to American measurements and available ingredients.

LA VINAIGRETTE DE PIGEONNEAU AUX PETITS LÉGUMES DE SAISON

Although Jean Pierre Silva offers this exquisite dish as an appetizer, I've often ordered it as my main course, especially at lunch.

Be sure to prepare the stock a day before you plan to cook

the dish. And remember to take the squab filets and legs from the refrigerator one hour before cooking.

Makes 4 servings.

4 cups (about 1 pound) baby vegetables, such as finger carrots, asparagus, zucchini, yellow squash and pearl onions
2 tablespoons unsalted butter
1 tablespoon vegetable oil
8 squab legs (reserved from stock) with skin attached—1 ounce each (see recipe for squab stock)
8 boneless squab filets (breast halves reserved from stock) with skin attached—2 ounces each (see recipe for squab stock)
¼ cup Sherry vinegar
⅓ cup squab stock (recipe, page 135)
¼ cup walnut oil

1. Steam each vegetable separately and then keep warm in the steamer, off the heat. As they steam, test for doneness using the following guide as a base: peeled 2½-inch finger carrots, 5–8 minutes; asparagus, 2–3 minutes; trimmed 1½-inch zucchini, 3 minutes; trimmed 2-inch yellow squash, 3 minutes; peeled ½-inch pearl onions, 5 minutes.

2. You will need a medium bowl or a double boiler hot and ready before starting, to complete the sauce. If using a bowl, choose a thick ceramic one and fill it with boiling water; empty and dry thoroughly when ready to complete the sauce. If using a double boiler, simply place over simmering water. Heat four dinner plates and a small platter in a 225° F. oven.

3. Combine the butter and vegetable oil in a heavy medium-size enamel or stainless-steel skillet over moderate heat. When very hot, add the squab legs and increase the heat slightly. Cook until crisp and golden brown, about 2 minutes. Turn with tongs and cook about 1 minute longer, until medium rare. Place on the hot platter and cover with aluminum foil. Add the breast halves, skin side down, to the skillet and cook until crisp and golden brown, about 3 minutes. Turn and cook until medium rare, 1–2 minutes. Combine with the legs on the hot platter.

4. Tilt the pan and carefully spoon and discard all but about 1 tablespoon of the fat, taking care to leave the brown particles

in the pan. Add the vinegar and deglaze the pan, scraping the bottom for 30 seconds. Add the squab stock and simmer over moderate heat, watching carefully as you stir, until reduced to ¼ cup (you will have to pour it into a measuring cup to tell).

Scrape the sauce into the hot dry bowl or double boiler. Using a hand-held electric mixer or a whisk, gradually beat in the walnut oil. The sauce will emulsify as you add the oil. Taste for flavor. If a stronger vinegar flavor is desired, beat in a few drops more vinegar.

5. On a cutting board, cut the breasts into thin slices. Arrange breast slices and 2 legs in a fan shape on each heated dinner plate and add ¼ of the vegetables to each. Spoon sauce over and serve hot.

SQUAB STOCK

Because this stock must simmer for 8 hours, start it a day before you plan to use it. Made from the trimmings after you have cut up the squab for *la vinaigrette de pigeonneau,* it gives you twice as much as you will need. Freeze the remaining half in a small covered container to make the recipe a second time without having to take the time to make the stock again.

Makes ⅔ cup.

4 large fresh squab (12 ounces–1 pound each), cleaned and split
   but with feet left on
2 quarts cold water
1 cup dry white wine
1 medium yellow onion (4 ounces), sliced
¼ cup chopped carrot
¼ cup chopped celery
1 sprig parsley
1 medium leek (about 6 ounces)
½ large bay leaf
¼ teaspoon dried thyme

1. Rinse the squabs under cold running water. If heads are present, chop off with a sharp cleaver and discard. Using a small sharp knife, cut along the top of the breastbone of each squab.

Then cut along each side of the breastbone, working close to the bone to remove each breast half. Use your fingers if necessary to loosen them as you work. Cut each half away from the carcass. Leaving the skin attached to the breasts, reserve them. Disjoint the thighbones by bending them backward. Feel the thigh meat with your fingers and sever the thighs from the carcass so as much meat as possible is still attached to the thighs. Chop off the feet and save them for the stock. Do not separate the drumsticks from the thighs. Repeat with the remaining squabs. Wrap the 8 breast halves and 8 legs together and refrigerate for a day or two, until you are ready to make *la vinaigrette de pigeonneau*. At that time, remove from refrigerator and leave at room temperature for one hour before cooking.

2. Chop the squab carcasses roughly with a cleaver. Place the chopped carcasses and the feet in a 4-to-5-quart stock pot. Add the water, wine, onion, carrot, celery and parsley.

3. Trim off the root of the leek. Cut off and discard the green stem, leaving only a 4-to-5-inch length from the white of the leek (with some light green). Split the leek in half lengthwise and rinse it well. Place one half, cut side up, on your work surface and top with the half bay leaf and thyme. Add the remaining leek half, cut side down, and tie the bundle tightly together with string to make a *bouquet garni*. Add the *bouquet garni* to the stockpot and bring to a simmer over moderate heat, skimming off any foam that rises to the surface. Reduce the heat to very low and keep at a bare simmer for 8 hours. The bubbles should only occasionally rise to the surface as it simmers.

4. Place a colander over a large bowl and pour the stock through. Shake the colander up and down and press on the contents with a spoon. Discard the solids. Pour the stock through a sieve (or a cheesecloth-lined sieve) to strain it once more. Let the stock cool to room temperature. The stock must be degreased; either refrigerate it until the fat on top congeals and then scrape off the fat and discard it, or use a special stock-degreasing cup with a spout at the bottom to separate the stock from the fat. You will have about 6 cups of degreased stock. (Don't be concerned if you have less, but if you do, the time it takes later to reduce to ⅔ cup will be less.)

5. To intensify the stock, place it in a medium saucepan and

boil gently until reduced to ⅔ cup, about 40 minutes. Cool to room temperature. Unless using right away, cover and refrigerate.

JAMBONETTE DE GRENOUILLES, ESTOUFFADE DE JEUNES POIREAUX

Jean Pierre Silva makes this dish of frogs' legs with wine lees, the strong-flavored sediment that settles to the bottom of a wine barrel. Because lees would be difficult, and in most cases impossible, to get here, we've adapted the recipe by infusing the *mirepoix* with several rapid reductions of red wine. It is not exactly the same, but it is still a delicious and intriguing dish.

If you like, split the pairs of legs and serve them as an hors d'oeuvre for 12 to 16 people.

Makes 4 servings.

8 young leeks (about 2 pounds)
¾ cup (1 ½ sticks) unsalted butter
½ cup finely chopped carrot
½ cup finely chopped shallots
¼ cup chopped parsley
2 cups red Burgundy wine
½ cup heavy cream
¼ teaspoon salt
16 pairs frogs' legs (2 pounds)
4 tablespoons all-purpose flour

1. Cut off the roots of the leeks and discard. Reserve the remaining stems. Cut the white portions with part of the light green into slices ¾ inch thick. Drop the slices into a bowl of cold water and rinse well. Drain and pat dry on paper towels.

2. Place 2 tablespoons of the butter in a heavy medium-size saucepan or sauté pan and melt over low heat. Add the sliced leeks, cover, and cook over low heat, shaking the pan occasionally, until they are tender, about 20 minutes. Do not let them color. Remove from the heat and keep warm in 225° F. oven.

3. Meanwhile, chop off and discard the darkest-green por-

tions of the leek stems. Cut the remaining medium-green portions lengthwise into quarters. Soak them in a large bowl of cool water to help dislodge the sand. Rinse well and pat dry. Chop into ½-inch pieces. You will need 3 cups for the sauce.

4. Melt 2 tablespoons of the remaining butter in a medium-size enamel or stainless-steel sauté pan or skillet over moderate heat. Add 3 cups chopped leek greens, the carrot, shallots and parsley; sauté for 5 minutes. Add ½ cup of the wine, increase the heat slightly and boil, stirring frequently, until the wine has evaporated (about 3 minutes). Add ½ cup more of the wine and cook until evaporated. Add another ½ cup wine and cook until evaporated. Finally, add the remaining ½ cup wine and the heavy cream and boil for 3 minutes. Remove from the heat.

5. Purée the mixture in a food processor or blender. Place a medium wire sieve over a bowl. Add the purée and force it through with the back of a spoon. Scrape any purée clinging to the bottom of the strainer into the sauce and discard the solids left in the strainer. Transfer the sauce (you will have about 1 cup) to a small enamel or stainless-steel saucepan. Stir in the salt, cover, and place in 225° F. oven to keep warm.

6. Cut the remaining 1 stick of butter into slices and place them in a small saucepan over moderate heat until melted. To clarify the butter, skim off the foam from the top with a spoon and carefully pour the clear butter into a cup, leaving behind the milky residue.

7. Soak the frogs' legs in a bowl of cool water for a few minutes and then rinse and drain them.

8. Place half of the clarified butter in a large heavy skillet over moderate heat.

9. Place 4 pairs of frogs' legs in a paper bag with 1 tablespoon of the flour. Shake to coat. Increase the heat under the skillet to moderately high and add the coated frogs' legs so the thickest parts are near the center of the pan. Fry, pressing with a spatula once in a while if they buckle, until crisp and golden, 3 to 4 minutes. Turn them with tongs and fry until done, about 3 minutes more. Drain on paper towels. Combine 4 more pairs of frogs' legs with 1 tablespoon of the remaining flour and coat and fry as before. Discard the butter and bits in the skillet and wipe it with paper towels. Using the remaining clarified butter, coat and cook the remaining frogs' legs in 2 sets of 4 pairs as before.

10. On each plate, serve 4 pairs of frogs' legs, ¼ of the leeks and ¼ of the sauce.

AILE ET CUISSE DE PINTADE À L'INFUSION DE THÉ, ZESTES D'ORANGES ET RIZ SAUVAGE

At Vieux Moulin, *pintade,* or guinea fowl, is the base of this dish. Because guinea fowl is not always readily found in the United States, we substituted pheasant when we adjusted the recipe for Americans. Pheasant, we found, blends beautifully with the flavors of tea, honey and orange, so depending on what is available, you can use guinea fowl or pheasant.

Be sure to prepare the stock a day before you plan to cook the dish. Remove the guinea fowl or pheasant pieces from the refrigerator an hour before you plan on cooking them.

Makes 4 servings.

Thin julienne strips of peel (zest) from 2 oranges
1 tablespoon loose-leaf Ceylon tea or two tea bags
1 cup boiling water
1 tablespoon honey
2 tablespoons unsalted butter
2 boneless pheasant or guinea fowl breast halves, reserved from
  stock (recipe, page 140)
2 pheasant or guinea fowl thighs reserved from stock
2 pheasant or guinea fowl drumsticks reserved from stock
¼ cup stock (see recipe)
¼ cup heavy cream

1. Bring a small pan of water to a boil and add the strips of orange peel. Blanch for 30 seconds and drain. Cover and reserve to garnish the dish.

2. Place the loose tea or tea bags in a cup and add the boiling water. Let steep for exactly 3 minutes. Strain or discard tea bags. Stir in honey and reserve until needed. Heat 4 dinner plates and a small platter in 225° F. oven.

3. Melt the butter in a large heavy skillet over moderate heat. Add the breasts and thighs, skin side down, and the drumsticks,

increase the heat slightly and cook until crisp and golden brown, about 5 minutes. Turn the pieces with tongs and cook 4–5 minutes longer, until just cooked through. Place the pieces on the hot platter and cover loosely with aluminum foil to keep warm.

4. Tilt the pan and carefully spoon off all but 2 tablespoons of the fat, taking care to leave the brown particles behind in the pan. Add the stock and deglaze the pan, stirring for 30 seconds. Add the tea and cream and bring to a boil over moderate heat. Boil, stirring frequently, until reduced to about ½ cup. The sauce will have a beautiful satin consistency.

5. Cut the breast halves in thin slices. Arrange the slices and one piece of thigh or drumstick in a fan shape on each of the heated dinner plates. Spoon the sauce over the meat and top with ¼ of the orange peel. Serve hot with wild rice.

PHEASANT OR GUINEA FOWL STOCK

The stock is made from the carcass of the pheasant or guinea fowl after the breasts, thighs and drumsticks have been removed, wrapped together and refrigerated. Substituting the pheasant or guinea fowl, follow the recipe for squab stock (see page 135). The stock will yield twice as much as you will need; freeze the remaining part in a covered container, and you will not have to make it the next time you prepare this dish.

POIRES AU VIN DE BOURGOGNE ET AUX ÉPICES

Fresh pears are poached in red Burgundy with spices and citrus fruits. The poaching wine is reduced to a light syrup. Jean Pierre Silva serves the pears and syrup with vanilla ice cream, but they are also delicious served alone.

Makes 6 servings.

6 firm pears (8 ounces each)
1 bottle red Burgundy wine
½ cup sugar
1 stick (about 3 inches long) cinnamon
6 whole peppercorns

½ large bay leaf
1 whole clove
2 slices lemon, about ¼ inch thick
2 slices orange, about ¼ inch thick

1. Choose a heavy medium-size enamel or stainless-steel saucepan that will hold the 6 pears snugly in an upright position.

2. Combine the wine, sugar, cinnamon, peppercorns, bay leaf, clove, lemon slices and orange slices in the saucepan. Bring to a boil over moderate heat. Simmer 5 minutes.

3. Meanwhile, slice away a thin sliver from the bottom of each pear so it will stand upright. With a swivel-bladed vegetable peeler, peel the pears. Stand them up in the simmering wine. Partially cover and simmer until tender when pierced with a skewer (20–30 minutes), spooning the wine over them on occasion as they poach. Remove the pan from the heat and let the pears cool completely in the liquid.

4. With a slotted spoon, transfer the pears to an attractive serving dish just large enough to hold them. Place a strainer over a medium-size enamel or stainless-steel pan and pour the poaching syrup through it. Discard the solids. Bring the syrup to a boil over moderate heat and boil until reduced to about ¾ cup or slightly less, about 15 minutes. The syrup should lightly coat a spoon. If a sweeter syrup is desired, add a little more sugar to taste and stir to dissolve it. Spoon the syrup over the pears. Cool to room temperature. Cover and refrigerate until well chilled. Serve cold.

18

INNOVATION AND YOUTH

❧

Their first joint effort was the Cannan & Wasserman wine list. Next, Le Serbet and Europvin combined the administrative aspect of their work on the Europvin computer. From there, the two companies moved to consolidate their total export system.

In Le Serbet's earliest days, service was basic and broad. Becky would ship a container, which holds about twelve hundred cases of twelve bottles each, to an importer. That container might have had cases of wine from as many as twenty different producers. Each producer sent a separate invoice to the importer, but while the importer received twenty invoices at about the same time, he did not necessarily pay twenty invoices at the same time.

Now Cannon & Wasserman sends one invoice to the importer for the entire container. The importer pays Cannan & Wasserman, which in turn pays the producers. "And if there's any delay in payment to us," Becky adds, "we still pay the producers immediately. We've built a good reputation with them, and we want to keep that reputation."

The joint system extends beyond invoicing. Take their Burgundy wines, as an example. Where Becky was once the person who went directly to a producer, it is now Dominique Lafon who makes the first visit to the cellar to taste.

"You might say I'm the first filter," he says. If the wine passes Dominique's test, he returns with Becky to taste. The final decision as to whether the wine will be put on the Cannan & Wasserman list is made when Becky, Dominique and Christopher Cannan taste as a team.

Once they choose a wine, they explain their system to the producer: They will send out an offer for the wine and/or list it in their catalog, in both cases with a reproduction of the label and a short description of the winemaker and wine, its appellation and prices. If an importer is interested and requests a sample of the wine, they air-freight a bottle to him. He tastes the wine. If he likes it, he orders it. The order is computerized at Europvin. A confirmation is sent to the producer. If the wine is to be shipped immediately, the producer receives a packet of label strips. If the wine is to be reserved for future shipment, the date is noted on the order.

The shipment of the wine involves many steps—and, often, missteps. An *acquit,* an official release paper for all alcoholic beverages, must be obtained from a *régie,* an excise office. A truck, whose license number must be on the *acquit,* can pick up the wine only within the hours and days stated on the *acquit.*

After the wine is loaded, the truck delivers it to a shipping company, such as Hillebrand, which specializes in transporting wines and spirits abroad. The wines are then loaded into a container.

The container is loaded into a ship, and the ship sails. If all goes well, the wine arrives, the importer receives it, he sells it and reorders.

"Then everyone is happy," Becky says. "People come to visit and say, 'Oh, I'd love to be a wine broker like you. You have so much fun—guests and dinners and you get to go to tastings all day.' Choosing the wine is a very small part of the business, only the beginning. Our daily bread depends on a thousand tiny details, like getting the right wine to the right place at the right time."

I drove to Pernand-Verglesses one day with Dominique to visit Roland Rapet. We waited while Monsieur Rapet finished racking his Corton-Charlemagne 1983. The wine was poured into a clean barrel while the café-au-lait-colored lees, the sediment that had settled to the bottom of the first barrel, were left behind. Lees are often used in cooking in Burgundy. For Monsieur Rapet, they serve another purpose: "I can tell a lot about a wine by seeing and smelling its lees." From his look of satisfaction, the lees of the Corton-Charlemagne were telling him very good things.

When he finished, the three of us went down into the *caves* and tasted through his 1982s, through four vintages of Aloxe-Corton and two of Le Corton. Later, upstairs, as we sat chatting, I asked him about his label, which, like so many in Burgundy, bears the family name and *"Père et Fils."*

"Which are you, Monsieur—*père* or *fils?"* I asked.

"I used to be the *fils.* Now I am the *père,* and I have a *fils;* he is twenty years old."

Père et *fils.* Father and son.

On our drive back to Bouilland, Dominique said, "There are so few *young* winemakers here in Burgundy. Mostly, there are only sons of fathers who are winemakers. How many young men in Burgundy are not working under their fathers; how many are doing everything or nearly everything themselves?"

Dominique's family has had its estate in Meursault since the end of the nineteenth century, when his great-grandfather Jules Lafon, a lawyer in Dijon, married Marie Boch. She brought with her ownership in a few vineyards, including the *Premier Cru* Meursault Genevrières; Monsieur Lafon bought more vineyards in Meursault *Premiers Crus* and a third of a hectare in Montrachet.

Jules Lafon's son Pierre died during World War II, when his own son René (Dominique's father) was only seventeen. René Lafon became an electrical engineer and worked away from Burgundy in his early years. But he always came to Meursault on his vacations to work at the domaine during the years his grandfather remained in charge of the estate. After the grandfather died, René's uncle took over the domaine, but he was pessimistic about its future. It doesn't work anymore, he told the family; it should be sold.

René Lafon did not agree. It was 1954, and although he had just begun to work in Paris, he decided to take charge of the domaine. For thirteen years, he spent the week in Paris, the weekend in Meursault. He planted and replanted and took his vacation each year at harvest time. He hired Henri Belorgey and put him in charge of the cellars; it was Monsieur Belorgey who showed the child Dominique how to use a press, how to rack wine, how to do many of the cellar operations. The vineyards were all under the *métayage* system.

In 1967, when Dominique was nine years old, the family moved from Paris to Meursault.

"When I was growing up, I played in the cellar, followed Monsieur Belorgey while he did his work and helped my father. But wine was for fun. I'd had it all my life. I didn't taste it seriously. It was only after I went to Dijon to study that I began to taste other people's wines and to understand how good ours were.

"It used to be that the father was the sole teacher. Now it's becoming the tradition for the son to go to school to study grape growing and winemaking and *then* to work with his father.

"And that changes things. At school, we learn not only about modern oenology but also about other people's wines. Take my family, for example. My father is a very intelligent man and, as you know, he lived in Paris and other places before moving back to Meursault. Still, I went to school in Dijon and in Beaune, I went to California, and now I meet with winemaking friends my own age to taste with them, and so I've probably tasted more wines—and I'm still in my twenties—than my father has in his lifetime. And my father is more sophisticated than many of my friends' fathers, so it is even more true of them."

Dominique's tasting group began when a few of his friends got together to talk about such subjects as viticulture, winemaking and the economics of running an estate. After one meeting, a young man said to another, "I never tasted at your estate. May I . . . ?" And the tasting group grew from there.

"We're a good-sized group now," Dominique said. "Étienne Grivot, the son of Jean Grivot in Vosne-Romanée; Étienne is the winemaker and makes about 90 percent of the decisions at that estate and at his aunt's estate, Domaine Jacqueline Jayer. Christophe Roumier, whose father is a winemaker in Chambolle-Musigny. Frédéric Lafarge; he's an exceptional taster. Natalie Pons and her brother Vincent; their family owns Domaine Pons in Volnay and the restaurant Cellier Volnaysien. Sophie Rossignol, the daughter of Jacques Rossignol of Domaine Trapet in Gevrey-Chambertin. And Chantal Michelot of Domaine Michelot in Meursault. We usually meet once a week in winter, each time at a different domaine."

Dominique also belongs to another group, smaller and more informal, whose members are Étienne Grivot, Patrick Bize of Domaine Bize in Savigny-lès-Beaune, Christophe Roumier and, until late 1984, Ted Lemon.

Possibly more than anyone, Ted Lemon symbolizes that change in Burgundy's tradition is indeed possible. Born in New York State, Ted went to Brown University in Providence to major in French literature, and in his junior year he spent six months at the University of Dijon. It was during his stay in Dijon that he really discovered wine. He met vintners, among them Jacques Seysses of Domaine Dujac in Morey-Saint-Denis, a former Parisian who is himself a rarity in Burgundy, having bought his first vineyards there only in 1967. He has since added to them, to form an enviable twenty-eight-acre domaine and a fine reputation for his wines.

By the time Ted had completed his semester in Dijon, some of his new friends suggested he stay on. "I said no." The slim, blond young man laughed. "Can you believe it?"

After he returned to Brown and finished his senior year, Ted applied for a Samuel T. Arnold Fellowship, which is offered by the International Business Machines Corporation and grants six thousand dollars for a year of postgraduate study or travel abroad.

"In my application, I said I wanted to go to Burgundy to learn winemaking," Ted said. "I was given a fellowship. I guess they like slightly risky projects."

In the fall of 1980, Ted was back at the University of Dijon, this time to study winemaking. During that year, he apprenticed at Domaine Dujac and other wine domaines. After he received his degree, he went to Hollister, California, to work with Josh Jensen at Calera Winery.

Meanwhile, in Meursault, Guy Roulot was dying. As the third generation of his family to head its domaine, Monsieur Roulot had been responsible for building the estate's present reputation. He bought more vineyards within the Meursault village appellation. He was one of the first *vignerons* in Meursault to keep wines made from the grapes of each vineyard separate

Ted Lemon.

and to label each of these village appellations under its vineyard name—Les Luchets and Les Tessons, for example. At the time of his death, Guy Roulot left an estate of nearly thirty-five acres and a good name for his wines.

Monsieur Roulot had a son, Jean-Marc, who had apprenticed at Joseph Phelps Vineyards in Napa Valley and had returned to work with his father. But Jean-Marc's love was the theater, not the wine cellar, and he left Meursault to study at the National Conservatory of Dramatic Arts in Paris.

Soon after Guy Roulot died, his wife, Geneviève, and his son began to search for another winemaker. One of the people whose advice they asked was Jacques Seysses.

"Of all the apprentices I've had, and I've had many," Jacques Seysses told Madame Roulot, "none has been as bright and as capable as Ted Lemon. He has so many fine qualities, but there are two problems. He is twenty-five years old, and he is American."

"Impossible," Madame Roulot said. Monsieur Seysses suggested she speak to other people she respected in Burgundy.

The family talked to Aubert de Villaine and to Patrick Bize, and Jean-Marc telephoned his friend Bruce Neyers at the Phelps winery, who knew Josh Jensen.

Late in 1982, Jacques Seysses called Ted Lemon at Calera. "How would you like to make Meursault?" In January 1983, Ted arrived at Domaine Roulot.

I met Ted when Dominique and I were tasting in Meursault one day. Domaine Roulot was our second stop, and as we went down the stairs into the cellar, we were speaking English. A young man was working near the barrels, and as he turned around, I said, *"Bonjour."*

"Hi," Ted Lemon answered.

As far as the people of Meursault remember—and their memories reach far back—Ted is the first American ever to be a winemaker in Burgundy. And their initial reaction when he arrived was one of deep surprise. Tradition, after all, dictated that son follow father. Why didn't Jean-Marc forget about the theater and follow his father? And if not the son, why not a relative or, at the very least, a fellow villager?

Ted spoke French fluently. "That helped," he said. "But at

first I had to prove myself physically to the cellar and field help. I had to prune as quickly, drive a tractor as well and work as hard as they could. And I had to prove to Madame Roulot, who was so devoted to Guy, that I could keep up the reputation of his wines."

He did. "People who don't fit into the tradition of Burgundy," Dominique said, "can be given a tough time. But Ted worked hard. He made very good wines. He was accepted."

Ted stayed in Burgundy for two years before going to California to begin another winemaking job. A few months before he left, I asked him why he had chosen Burgundy.

"To begin, why France? Because like the French, I believe soil is of major importance in a wine's character. It's clear there are tremendous differences between wines made from vineyards right next to each other even if they are vinified and treated exactly the same way. Why Burgundy? Because it's more open than the aristocratic society of Bordeaux. It's easier to make contacts here.

"In another sense, though, Burgundy is more closed because it's so married to tradition. Father to son, father to son. But I'll tell you what gives me hope here. The young people. They're combining tradition with technical competence, and they're so highly motivated. As Dominique told you, he and I and a group of friends meet regularly to taste the wines of other growers. We learn from each other. That would rarely have happened a generation ago."

One tradition knocked slightly askew.

Beyond the new generation of winemakers, beyond the traditional *vigneron* family, the wine broker, the barrelmaker, the chef, there are many other lives in Burgundy that revolve around wine. There is the *négociant.* There are owners of famous domaines. There are owners of small or new or little-known domaines. Each adds a facet to the life of Burgundy. Each has a story.

19

AUBERT DE VILLAINE

The vineyard is called L'Hermitage and it is near Bouzeron, a small village in the part of Burgundy south of the Côte d'Or known as the Côte Chalonnaise. Until about one hundred years ago, when it was abandoned, the vineyard surrounded a four-teenth-century stone church and an earlier stone hut where, over the generations, one hermit after another lived.

In 1974, Aubert de Villaine bought the four-and-a-half-acre wild field and tamed it by planting Pinot Noir and Aligoté. What he left undisturbed, on a rise in the center of the field, was a thicket of trees and tall grasses that surround a wall and, within the wall, the ruins of the church and the hut.

Late one hazy, hot June day, after walking past rows of vines, noting the more serrate leaves of the Pinot Noir, the rounder leaves and slightly redder wood of the Aligoté vines, we pushed our way through thigh-high grass, past trees, and climbed the stone wall.

From the wall, Aubert de Villaine looked down at the ruins, ancient stones that had long ago tumbled into their own founda-tions. The fields, the hills around us, seemed endlessly big. The silence became almost tangible, and soon all our afternoon's talk about grapes and wine, soil and rootstock, new cellars and new appellations, evaporated. "I feel such peace here," Aubert said. "I can easily put myself in the spirit of the hermit. I can under-stand why he felt this is a good place, perhaps the best place, to be alone."

Aubert de Villaine, however, is rarely alone. He is co-director, with Lalou Bize-Leroy, of Domaine de la Romanée-Conti. With his wife, Pamela, he has created and owns A. et P. de Villaine, a forty-two-acre wine domaine centered in Bouzeron. He is deputy mayor of the village of Bouzeron. He is the originator of a new appellation for Bouzeron, and he has now formed a committee to introduce a proposal for another appellation for the area.

Yet despite his very engaged twentieth-century life, the tall, slender, dark-eyed de Villaine, with his deep, resonating voice and patrician good looks, seems never to forget the roots of the land. In the vineyards, in the winery, in talks about Burgundy, one religious figure particularly weaves his way into and around Aubert de Villaine's thoughts. And that is the medieval monk.

"Just think of the Côte d'Or's hills; if you plant anything but vines on them, they will give very little. It was the monks who discovered that each part of the hills was different from the others, each part grew grapes that made a different wine. It is because the monks understood these differences that Burgundy looks like stained glass, with its small patches of vineyards.

"The marriage between a grape varietal and where it is planted was not a thing that had to be decided. In Burgundy, it was shaped over the centuries. In that way, Burgundy has stayed closest to what God has decided.

"Isn't it unbelievable to think that nothing has really changed since the time of the monks? There was wine before them, yes, but it was they who first created great wines here. If you think that these great wines began in the twelfth century, and if you say that each person has lived an average of fifty years, then it is only about sixteen lifetimes since we've had these great wines. It is not such a long time."

The de Villaine family has been involved with the great wines of Burgundy for a few of those lifetimes. It began in the 1830s, a time of crisis in Burgundy, when the cellars were filled with barrels of unsold wine. Some years, the situation became so acute that one vintage of wine had to be thrown away to make room for the next. But one man, a grape grower and wine merchant, saw the situation as an opportunity. The market would change, he reasoned, and so Monsieur Duvault-Blochet borrowed money and bought wine. Two years later, when Burgundy became fashionable again, he sold his wine and made a small fortune. With it, he began to buy vineyards. Among them were those of Domaine de la Romanée-Conti, which he acquired in the 1860s. At the time of his death, Monsieur Duvault-Blochet owned more than six hundred acres; they were divided among his heirs.

The heirs left their inheritances to heirs, and through the generations, Aubert's branch of the family came to own 50 percent of Domaine de la Romanée-Conti. Slowly, however, members of other branches of the family began to sell their part of the inheritance.

Aubert's great-uncle Jacques Chambon sold his half of the Domaine in 1942 to Henri Leroy. And in the 1960s, the last great sale of the original property was completed when Aubert's cousins the de LaVoreilles sold Pousse d'Or in Volnay. (Jacques Seysses' father is one of the new owners of that domaine.) Today, five generations after the death of Monsieur Duvault-Blochet, only Aubert's family has retained its part of the original vineyards.

Domaine de la Romanée-Conti today consists of nearly 50 acres: all of the vineyard Romanée-Conti (4½ acres), all of La Tâche (about 15 acres), and parts of Richebourg (about 8⅔ acres), Grands Échézeaux (8⅔ acres), Échézeaux (11⅓ acres) and Montrachet (about 1¼ acres). The Domaine also farms 13 acres of Romanée-Saint-Vivant. All but Montrachet are red-wine vineyards; and all but Montrachet are in the Côte de Nuits. Montrachet itself is a recent addition, having been acquired by purchases made in 1964, 1966 and 1980.

Most remarkably, all of the Domaine's vineyards are *Grands Crus*.

Aubert's own estate, A. et P. de Villaine, is quite another story. He bought the first part of the property, which was sixteen planted acres, in 1972, a year after he and Pamela Fairbanks were married. The wines he makes at Bouzeron are far simpler than those of Domaine de la Romanée-Conti. He knows the soil is different in his Côte Chalonnaise vineyards, and he knows he cannot use the same methods on his Chalonnais wine that are used at the Domaine.

"If I did the same things here, we'd have wines that were

Pamela and Aubert de Villaine at their domaine in Bouzeron.

harder and more powerful, but they would be less appealing. We would lose the character that can develop in wines here, and that is good fruit and grace and lightness." But Aubert did his apprenticeship at the Domaine, and among the things he learned there was the pursuit of quality. He follows that same principle in Bouzeron: in his Bourgogne Aligoté Bouzeron; in his Bourgogne "Les Clous," a Chardonnay named after its vineyard; his Bourgogne rouge; and his rosé of Pinot Noir.

Aubert de Villaine was born in 1939. "My parents planned to have the birth take place in Paris. But while they were vacationing in Normandy, where part of my father's family comes from, my mother fell. And so I was born in Normandy."

During World War II, his father was a prisoner of the Germans. "I didn't see him until I was five years old. I remember my mother telling me to be very nice to the man who was coming to our home because 'he is your father.' After he was with us for two weeks, I said to her, 'He's nice. When will he go?'

"My mother is Russian. Her parents left Russia, going first to Estonia and then to England in 1921. My grandfather had been in the last duma, the assembly under the czar. My grandmother was one of the five ladies-in-waiting to the czarina. When they arrived in England, my grandfather must have been about forty-eight years old, my grandmother, about forty-three. He was a broken man after exile. But my grandmother—what an extraordinary woman. She worked in England, making a living by giving Russian lessons. 'I've never been so happy as I am now,' she'd say. She drew a line between the end of one part of her life and the beginning of a new life. She was the epitome of the *grande dame;* she had no weaknesses, not one. She believed in gaiety and good spirits, and she had tremendous discipline. She was a great example for me."

Aubert and his family lived in Moulins—about seventy-five miles from Burgundy—where his father was a banker. Then, in 1952, his French grandfather, who had been managing Domaine de la Romanée-Conti, died, and Aubert's father, Henri, took over. For all its fame, the Domaine during the years of Aubert's father and grandfather, and even before that, was never really profitable. It was a kind of grand prize that offered little income. And both Aubert's grandfather and father wanted—indeed, needed—to do other kinds of work; neither wanted total involvement in vineyards.

Aubert attended school in Moulins until he was thirteen and then went off to boarding school near Paris. Later, at the university, he studied Greek and literature and also went to law school.

Through an introduction by Colonel Frederick Wildman, he met Louis Benoist, who owned Almadén Vineyards in California. After he finished his studies, Aubert went to California for sixteen months; he spent most of his stay at Almadén. "Louis Benoist was a man of exceptional quality. I worked for him in the harvest and in the offices. I rode horseback through the vineyards with Professor Albert Winkler of the University of California's school of oenology at Davis. Until recently, I still wore the Stetson I had at Almadén. It was covered with oil from working on my own tractor here. I remember meeting Bob Mondavi in Napa Valley when he was still at Charles Krug Winery with his family. I discovered a new life in California; it was a very happy time."

Aubert began writing articles about California wines in 1965, possibly the first Frenchman to do so. They were published in *Revue du Vin de France.* "At that time, France knew nothing about California wines. I was fascinated with the passion of the people making them. When I think what those wines were like in the 1960s and what they are today, it is unbelievable. I don't think even Bob Mondavi knew then what California wines would become.

"The major difference I see between the birth of wine in California and in our region is that we are living with a creation that was begun hundreds of years ago without one bit of commercial necessity. The monks used the wine for themselves, for guests, to give as gifts, but not for commerce. In California, commerce is behind every winery. The destiny of a region built with a necessity for profit will be different from the destiny of a region that began without a need for profit. Today, you could not create Burgundy."

Aubert was always very close to the Domaine, but it was only after he returned from the United States in 1965 that he decided

[155]

he wanted to work there. His father and Lalou Bize-Leroy's father were co-directors.

"When I first joined the Domaine, I worked in the vineyards and the winery, and for three years I also worked with Maison Leroy, the *négociant,* to gain sales experience."

It was during a business trip to the United States for the Domaine in 1969 that he met Pamela Fairbanks. A native of Pasadena, California, Pamela had gone to Mount Vernon Junior College in Washington, D.C., and then, in 1962, to Paris to attend L'Académie Maxim's, which offered a year's study of French culture.

When the course ended, Pamela stayed on to study art history at the École du Louvre. She did not return to San Francisco—where her mother, widowed and remarried, now lived—until 1965. But she did not stay in San Francisco for long. She returned to Paris for another year of study, this time at the Musée des Arts Décoratifs in Paris. In 1968, she moved to New York to work at *House Beautiful.*

Meanwhile, Lynne Wildman, Freddy Wildman's cousin and a friend of Pamela's, suggested to some friends that they contact Aubert de Villaine when they were in France. They did, and in turn they suggested that Aubert contact Pamela when he was in New York. In March of 1969, when he was passing through New York, Aubert de Villaine called Pamela Fairbanks.

"I will return to New York next Saturday. Will you have dinner with me?"

"We had dinner at the Russian Bear," Pamela remembers. "Aubert's mother is Russian, you know. Aubert was staying with Freddy Wildman's parents. It was a wonderful evening. We met a few more times before he returned to France."

A few months later, Pamela went to France. And a few months after that, she went to France again. In August 1970, Aubert went to California to meet Pamela's family, and they became engaged.

In March of 1971, they were married in Vosne-Romanée. As is the French custom, there was first a civil ceremony, conducted by the village mayor. Madame Gros had just been elected, and theirs was the first ceremony she performed. The next day, Pamela and Aubert had their church wedding. Becky Wasserman's harpsichord was taken to the church, and though she was there as a guest, not as a musician, it was her instrument that filled the church with music. It was at the wedding that Becky and Bart Wasserman first met Freddy Wildman.

Pamela and Aubert lived in Beaune in his bachelor apartment while they looked for a house, but they could find nothing suitable on the Côte d'Or. Then Aubert heard about a property in the village of Bouzeron, near the town of Chagny, on the Côte Chalonnaise. It consisted of sixteen planted acres, a house, and an old winery and cellar. The oldest part of the house had been built somewhere between the sixteenth and seventeenth centuries. The rest was added on about a hundred years ago. "But it has no real style," Aubert says of the house. "Bouzeron has always been a rather poor village and so the house was built with chestnut beams, which are less expensive than oak." Aubert and Pamela looked around the property. They could see how much work it needed, what a difficult life it would be, what a tremendous undertaking it was. And they said to each other, "Why not?" Before 1972 ended, they bought it.

"Aubert and everyone else worried about my adjusting to country living in Bouzeron," Pamela says, "but really, the most difficult thing was people saying to me, 'It will be difficult.' Yes, there was one thing, and that was getting my driver's license. I had never before driven a standard shift, and at the beginning I rode my bicycle everywhere.

"Cooking was a bigger problem. Before I married, my family would say the only thing I had ever cooked were lamb chops, and I burned them. Once, in San Francisco, my brother brought me a hibachi. I put it on a glass-topped table and began to make hamburgers on it. The hibachi crashed through the glass, and so I can't even say I made hamburgers successfully."

Becky and Bart Wasserman helped change that. Their wedding gift to Pamela was cooking lessons with their own cook, Madame Rondet.

"Between Madame and Becky, I learned," Pamela says. "But I still think of myself as Babar the elephant in the kitchen. I prefer gardening."

Despite her protests, the slim, agile, dark-haired Pamela cooks well and often. There are visitors throughout the year.

And there are the harvest meals to prepare. "Friends usually come down in August, and for most of the week we cook—stews, vegetable mousses, soups, cakes. Then I freeze it all for the *vendange,* when I have to feed thirty-five to forty pickers twice a day."

But years before they needed three dozen pickers to help with the harvest, there was a domaine to create. "Often, in those early days, we didn't sleep nights, worrying," Pamela said. "But we've built it up. And we've added to it. It's something we've done together."

For Aubert, it meant working in the vineyards, planting and tending vines, harvesting, making wine.

"We've slowly replanted almost everything on our original property. Slowly, we bought more land—the unplanted Appellation Contrôlée fields, L'Hermitage and La Fortune, and other small fields. I had to borrow money to do it. And for the first three years, we did not bottle any wine. Financially, it was a very difficult time. I was working very hard at Bouzeron, and at the same time I worked at the Domaine. I was fortunate to have a good foreman here, Valentin de Sousa from Portugal.

"But working here, creating it, has been very satisfying. Here, small things make great changes. At the Domaine, we can make only small adjustments to maintain it; there, it's artist's work.

"Since my father retired in 1975 and I have become co-director of the Domaine, I have little time to do fieldwork here. And I'm sorry about that. I love to work in the vineyards. I remember when I was working out there full-time. We'd stop in the morning at 9 A.M., burn vine cuttings, catch some snails crawling in the vineyards and roast them. Then we'd add a bit of salt and eat them. Delicious!

"I am the last one of the family to own the vineyards we inherited. And I am perhaps the only member of the family to begin a vineyard as we have here in Bouzeron. But Burgundy is a place of continuity. Even if the Domaine were sold tomorrow, there would be little change. In order to produce the same wine, the new owners would have to do the same things we have been doing."

At the Domaine, Lalou Bize-Leroy and Aubert de Villaine

share the responsibility, with both of them involved in the vine-yards, winemaking, tasting and marketing. For the Domaine's cooperage, Aubert goes to the forests with the cooper Jean Fran-çois to choose wood. The Domaine uses only fine-grained oak from Tronçais. After it is selected and split, it is brought to Burgundy, to the village of Saint-Romain, where Tonnellerie François Frères is located, and kept separate from other oak for two years to dry outdoors, before being made into barrels.

"The Domaine orders barrels with no toast on the inside. Oak and great wine are a perfect marriage. With wines like Richebourg and La Tâche, for example, the wood acts as a set-ting, and the wine takes over. In lesser wines, though, the wood can take over."

As Aubert learned more about the wines of Bouzeron, he began to understand their quality and their history. He found that around the turn of the century, young Aligoté was greeted with the same kind of celebration and enthusiasm that greets Beaujolais Nouveau today. He learned that in Paris between the world wars, the bistro across from the Gare de Lyon put up a sign each November: "Come get your Aligoté de Bouzeron." And he read that even back in the nineteenth century, Aligoté was sold under the name Bouzeron. There were indeed characteris-tics about Aligoté made in Bouzeron that were different—and better—than Aligoté made in other parts of Burgundy. And yet there was only one regional appellation—Bourgogne Aligoté.

For four years, Aubert de Villaine worked to secure a sepa-rate appellation for the Aligoté of Bouzeron. To create a new appellation requires a new law approved by the government; it is not easy to obtain. Aubert organized a committee of the grow-ers of Bouzeron. He did historical research. His committee in-vited official commissions to come to Bouzeron to taste the wines. In March 1979, the new appellation was approved. It is Bourgogne Aligoté de Bouzeron, and it makes Bouzeron the only commune with its own appellation for this white wine.

With that victory secured, he has begun another appellation project. "The appellation Bourgogne rouge is very large, cover-ing the area of the Yonne, the Côte d'Or and the Saône et Loire areas. It even includes Gamay, because the *Crus* of Beaujolais can be declassified to Bourgogne rouge. In such a large expanse, there is a great deal of difference between wines and a great deal of mediocre wine. On the Côte d'Or, for example, it includes all the lesser Pinot Noir planted across the flatland on the east side of the road. "On the Côte Chalonnaise, our appellation Bourgogne rouge is more noble because it grows on good slopes and produces low yields and makes the best red wines of the village. But because there is only one large appellation, our better wines suffer the reputation of the poorer wines."

So once again, Aubert has organized a committee to work at taking the good red wine of the Côte Chalonnaise out of the broad appellation and giving it its own Côte Chalonnaise appellation.

Along with his duties at the Domaine and at Bouzeron, Aubert is deputy mayor of this village of 151 people. France Lechenault has been mayor of Bouzeron since 1935, but since he is also a senator and spends much of his time in Paris, it often falls to Aubert to be at the mayor's office Monday and Friday from 6:30 to 8:00 P.M., when villagers come by to register complaints and ask for help.

Throughout the year, but especially in the spring and summer and fall, Pamela and Aubert entertain visitors from around the world. All through the year, there is vineyard work and cellar work to be done. And in the fall, all energies are turned to the harvest and the new wine. Pamela does her marketing in Chagny, just three miles away, where "there is a wonderful butcher, six bakeries and four flower shops." But Pamela de Villaine hardly needs a flower shop. Her own garden, her pride, is a beautiful rainbow of colors, of flowers and strawberries, of tomatoes, carrots, corn, squash and leeks, and of fresh thyme, sage, marjoram and winter savory.

Then winter comes, and the garden is quiet. "All through the rest of the year, I always say I cannot wait for winter so that I can catch up on my reading and on little chores," Pamela said late one fall day as we walked through the garden. "But winter is busy too."

Pamela has done wonderful things with the house that Aubert once claimed "has no real style." She has made an airy, homey space out of the large chestnut-beamed room that is the oldest part of the house. And in a small salon, she has created an intimate room with soft peach walls, a beige-and-peach rug, and comfortable chairs covered with a peach print.

"We have friends over for dinner in winter. There are always big fires in the fireplace. It's cozy.

"And there is our own Saint Vincent celebration for the patron saint of *vignerons* in January. On the Côte d'Or, the fête is held in a different village each year, but Bouzeron is not included. Bouzeron used to have its own celebration, but that stopped soon after the First World War. Then, in 1981, we decided to hold a special Saint Vincent mass. The next year it was suggested we add a *vin d'honneur,* an apéritif at a *vigneron*'s home, after mass, and that we carry a statue of the saint in a processional to the church, along with some giant brioches to be blessed. When we started this, the mayor asked the villagers if anyone remembered what had happened to the old flags of Saint Vincent. And yes, they did, some of the old people. One of them had preserved them in his attic. They needed patching—after all, they had been there since about 1920. Maria, who is a couturière and the daughter of a *vigneron,* mended them. Now we have a red-white-and-blue flag and a green velvet banner. They are kept in the mayor's cellar. In 1983, we added a banquet at one of the two local cafés to our celebration. The women and children make paper flowers and other decorations, and we decorate the house of the *vigneron* who is receiving guests that year. Of course, it usually rains or snows that day and the decorations are dripping. It is usually the middle Sunday in January. Such excitement. It is our midwinter celebration, our break. And soon, winter passes."

One evening, months after winter, Pamela, Aubert and I were having dinner. Aubert was especially pensive and reflected a long time before he spoke. "I was eating an apple this afternoon. A very good apple. It made me realize that to make a bad product is a sin. It is doing wrong with what's been given to us. It is a loss of respect for the natural thing."

And then this man, who seems to live every present moment aware of the past, added: "It was the monks who gave Burgundy its birth. We Burgundians must preserve what they made. I think there are enough people here who are conscious of that. This is, after all, a land of continuity."

[161]

As we said good night later in the evening, a full moon studded against a black sky beamed down on the silent little village. And like another moment, the day in L'Hermitage vineyard, the edges of time and distance, size and motion, seemed to soften and envelop each other. Perhaps Aubert's thoughts were on the ruins of the hermit's hut. Perhaps they were on the medieval monks. "There is something divine about Burgundy, don't you think?" he said.

20

LALOU BIZE-LEROY

The mountains were her first challenge. And nearly twenty-seven years after Lalou Bize-Leroy made her first ascent, the challenge is still there. It is not so much to climb the highest peak, she is quick to point out, as it is to take the toughest route up to that peak. But even as that route is met and mastered, there is only a chimera of success. There is, after all, another peak, another route. The challenge remains.

"There is no such thing as success," Madame Bize-Leroy will insist. "It is illusionary. If you search for quality, for perfection, the best is always still to be discovered. In the mountains and in wine."

In the world of wine, she is director of Maison Leroy, *négociants* headquartered in the Côte de Beaune village of Auxey-Duresses. She is also co-director of Domaine de la Romanée-Conti in Vosne-Romanée. Leroy is not the largest *négociant* in Burgundy, but there are few, if any, others that can match its wine collection—over three million bottles, which include many of the greatest *Premier Cru* and *Grand Cru* wines of Burgundy, with those for sale dating back to 1933, and others, not for sale, dating to 1929. While Lalou shares ownership of Maison Leroy with other members of her family, it is she, as director, who is absolute ruler of day-to-day operations.

Romanée-Conti is not the largest domaine in Burgundy, but there is none that approaches it for fame or, for that matter, the price of its wine. At the Domaine, Madame Bize-Leroy shares responsibility equally with Aubert de Villaine.

Reed slim and of medium height, Lalou Bize-Leroy is a woman who combines fierce energy with lean-limbed elegance and suave sophistication, a woman who carries fine clothes, athletic prowess and blatant power with equal ease. The keen athletic ability is attuned to the mountains. The power is the result of resilient strength and tough business maneuverings in the wine trade. The energy is unbounded, so that it feeds her professional life and leaves great quantities for her husband and daughter.

It was Lalou's great-grandfather François Leroy who began Maison Leroy in 1868, when he acquired the seventeenth-century cellars of the Boillot family in Auxey-Duresses. Toward the end of the 1800s, his son, Joseph, took over and developed the small business considerably, buying some of Burgundy's great wines in their infancy and keeping them in the Leroy cellars to age. In 1919, Joseph's son Henri entered the business and he remained active in the wine trade until the morning of his death, in February 1980.

Henri had no sons to whom he could pass on Maison Leroy. There was Pauline, his elder daughter, who later married an entrepreneur. And there was Lalou, the younger child, who adored her father as far back as she has a memory. "When I was three years old, I remember wanting to be with my father when he was discussing business with his clients. Even as a child I remember loving the tastes and smells of wine, loving the celebration of wine, but I never thought of entering the wine business."

Lalou, who was born in Paris, grew up in Burgundy. At the Sorbonne, she earned a degree in German and a license to teach; she also studied Latin, Greek and Spanish.

It was after graduation that she became interested—obsessed, really—with mountain climbing. "I had skied in the mountains, but I had never made an ascension. I began to dream of climbing. Then, one holiday, I was in the mountains with five friends. I wanted so much to climb, but one friend had a headache, another a knee problem. Finally, at 3 A.M., I left, alone. I was so excited. It was Monte Rosa near Zermatt.

"The next week, my friends and I climbed Aiguille Verte in Couloir Nymper, near Mont Blanc. And from there, little by little, I built up my climbing. Very soon, I thought only of mountains. I could not live without mountain climbing. My parents were very worried."

She had many suitors at the time, and for a while, she was engaged to be married. She broke the engagement when her choice of mate displeased her father. But by then, she realized she could only marry a man who shared her passion for mountains.

"I thought that the only thing that would make me happy would be to move to the mountains and spend my life climbing, teaching others to climb, and mastering every peak by the hardest route."

But her adored father had other plans for her. He wanted her to join the family wine business. In April 1955, when she was twenty-three years old, her father appointed her director of Maison Leroy, "Gardien des Grands Millésimes"—Guardian of the Great Vintages—as its catalog says.

"But director of what?" she says now. "Of nothing. From the time of my grandfather, there was only some marc and cassis left. My father had bought wine and there were a few old bottles in the cellar, but mostly, he treated Maison Leroy more as a hobby than as a business. He had purchased half of Domaine de la Romanée-Conti in 1942 from Jacques Chambon, a great-uncle of Aubert de Villaine, and he concentrated almost all his efforts on it rather than on Maison Leroy."

As the new director of that "sleeping business," as she called it, Lalou Leroy was determined to build it up. "It was difficult, very difficult at first, because no one believed in Leroy then. I decided to give myself to it, to make it important."

With the volcanic energy and all-consuming passion that helped her master mountains, and a feline sharpness that has awed many people in the wine trade since, Lalou went about upgrading Maison Leroy. She tasted and studied. She trained herself to identify the vineyard from which the grapes of each wine came. She worked until she was as qualified as anyone in the Burgundy wine trade. And she began to buy wine for Maison Leroy—current vintages and also such exalted older years as 1949, 1945, 1935. "All the good ones," she says.

Meanwhile, climbing remained her other passion. Certainly,

there were men in her life, suitors who hummed about her, but "there was no one whom I loved enough to give up either my wine business or my mountain climbing."

And then she met Marcel Bize. A Swiss champion skier and a typographer by trade, Marcel was also an excellent climber.

They were married in June 1960, and he left his native Switzerland to live in Burgundy with Lalou.

"When we met, he did not drink wine. Not a drop, because he thought it might be harmful. But I gave him La Tâche '45, and he liked it," Lalou said, flashing one of her dazzling smiles, which give a luminescence to her large, wide-set blue eyes.

Lalou and Marcel Bize and their daughter, Perrine, live at Domaine d'Auvenay, a twelfth-century estate where corn, colza (a forage crop) and other agricultural products are grown. Wild mushrooms abound. So do animals—hare, pheasant, boar, deer.

"We love animals very, very much," Lalou said, "so we have set aside the entire estate as a game reserve. *No* hunting—ever —is allowed on our property."

Marcel manages the 865-acre estate. Tall, trim, distinguished, he is as much the master of it as Lalou is mistress of her wine trade.

Like many of the better *négociants,* Maison Leroy owns some vineyards—a little over eleven acres in Auxey-Duresses, Meursault, Pommard, Musigny, Chambertin and Clos de Vougeot. For the rest of her stock, Lalou Bize-Leroy buys wine. "Always wine, not grapes. If you buy wine, you know what it will be.

"I have an ideal for each wine, for each area. I hope it will be the right wine for other people, but I never select wine just to please one person or another.

"Because I produce wine, I know what it is to be told, 'Your wine is no good.' I cannot do that to other producers; I find it impossible. So when I want to buy wine, a few *courtiers,* intermediaries, who know the kind of wine I like and how I taste, collect samples and bring them to me. If I buy them, then the producer knows it is for Maison Leroy. If I don't buy them, he never knows who tasted his wines. Once the wines are bought, they are put into our cellars—we have four cellars here in Auxey-Duresses, and others in Meursault, Rully and Borgy. Leroy always has two or three vintages in cask in the cellars. Wines need

Lalou Bize-Leroy in the cellars of Maison Leroy in Auxey-Duresses.

cold to make them strong, and so they must be kept through at least two winters."

While most Leroy wines stay in wood a minimum of two years, it is not a fast rule. "The wine orders the time in wood; I don't," Madame Bize-Leroy says. "Some wines need new oak, others don't. If a wine comes from old vines, for example, then it does not always need new barrels. I know it's fashionable now to use new oak, but oak is like makeup on a woman. If a woman is good-looking, she doesn't need much makeup. Oak is a cosmetic for wine.

"You must understand, too much oak can be a fault. In wine, the *terroir,* the soil, is of prime importance. No one has the right to impose another character on it. I think of oak as I do of pepper in the kitchen. A little enhances; too much ruins a dish.

"We rack our wines once. When I buy, I may rack them to transport them to my cellar. Usually, that's all. We fine our red wines with egg whites and our white wines with skim milk. Occasionally, we filter our whites, but we do not generally filter our reds. We do as little to the wine as possible."

But to return to buying wine. What does Madame Bize-Leroy look for in a wine? How does she judge a wine? How does she choose a few from the hundreds of samples of young wine brought to her?

"First, I look to identify the *terroir.* Where were the grapes grown and do they represent that vineyard? The wine must speak for its *terroir.* I look for the fruit. I look for the health of the wine. To age well, a wine must be healthy; it must have enough acidity and tannin and strength."

She knows wines primarily by their *terroir,* and she judges them on how true they are to their vineyard. "Each wine has its own character. A Chambolle-Musigny must be delicate, light. Corton must be strong. Pommard is *carré,* square; it is not by chance that the church in the village of Pommard is square. You find often that the houses and the people of a village are like the wines of the village. Certainly, the people of Volnay are not like the people of Auxey-Duresses. In Volnay, they are more refined, less open, almost austere. In Auxey-Duresses, they are a bit rough, coarse, but goodhearted and simple."

There are also the distinctions between vintages, and as all wine people know, even in great vintages some poor wines are made, and each poor vintage yields some good wines.

"I bought very few wines in 1975," Madame Bize-Leroy says, blue eyes flashing under her short-cropped blond hair. "It was a very poor year. No Pommard, no Auxey-Duresses; they weren't good enough. But I did choose some nice Clos Saint-Denis. I was told 1977 was not good, but I have some superb wines from that harvest. Both 1973 and 1974 were poor years; yet I selected a few good wines. Wines from poor vintages need more time in bottle to develop. We buy some kinds of wines for early development. We buy other wines for late development. And the wines of a great harvest we always hold till maturity."

Along with high quality standards, many of the wines of Maison Leroy are in fact known for their longevity. "Ideally, after bottling, I would like to hold most of my wines for twenty years. Sometimes it is difficult. I must learn every day to have patience. But my 1964s are only ready now, in 1984. This morning, I tasted six *Premier Cru* Meursault of 1969. They are fine, but they could be better; they are still too young. The Meursault Perrières, in particular, are not ready. The Meursault Perrières of other *vignerons* are different. Some are ready; some are already dead. My '78s are fruity and nice, of course, but they are like children. They have nothing to tell us yet. The *terroir* is the soul, the spirit of wine, and when a wine is young, the *terroir* is not so well expressed. It is exactly like a young person; he is not yet molded, not yet educated. Here, let us sample a one-year-old Pommard and a ten-year-old Pommard. You taste the difference?

"The ten-year-old has heart; it is the *terroir.* That's why I like older wines; their character has developed.

"But no one can really tell you how long a wine will live. When people ask me, for example, 'How long will your '82s live?' I answer, 'How tall will your children grow?' "

Lalou Bize-Leroy's office is filled with photographs—of her husband and daughter, her father and mother, and of herself and mountains and animals. But she waves a hand at it, a sturdy, workmanlike hand with long fingers that end in short, unadorned nails. "I am rarely in it." The reception room near the entrance has a fireplace, a mirror above it, reprints of articles about Lalou, and more photographs.

Sometimes, in my visits with her, we have sat in the office, but most often we have been in the reception room, which is like an elegant sitting room in a country estate. And at other times, we have gone down to the cellars to taste and talk. Lalou leads the way, with a long, determined stride, often wearing pants—perhaps sleek leather, perhaps well-tailored wool—always with high-heeled pumps, always chic, always followed by Freddy, a big, friendly black mongrel that Lalou found, abandoned, as a pup.

The cellars, like all Burgundian cellars, are cold. But once Lalou begins to taste, she seems to enter another realm, never complaining of the bone-chilling dampness. She tastes nearly every day, averaging perhaps forty, fifty wines. She learned wine and the wine trade by tasting, and like an athlete training to keep in top form, she rarely misses a day. Barrel after barrel is tasted. Bottle after bottle is perched on an empty upright barrel, poured and tasted. No wine is wasted. What is not drunk is poured back. She bristles slightly when a buyer says her wines are expensive. She does not deny that they are. "Quality is never cheap." No one who has dealt with her professionally claims she is soft and gentle. Rather, she is often described as shrewd and inflexible. But when the bargain is sealed—with an importer, a restaurateur —the charming, sensuous Lalou appears. The brilliant smile flashes. The tough, driving _négociant_ becomes a warm, caring woman.

The loving Lalou is the woman in her. The often unyielding wine director, it has been said, is the Henri Leroy in her. Lalou's father was an astute businessman who amassed a fortune in vineyards and wine, and, according to some people, gave no quarter. "He was intractable," I have often been told.

But there are other impressions of Henri Leroy. "So many growers have spoken of him with the highest respect," Becky Wasserman said. "They've told me, 'We would never think of taking anything to him but the best cuvées.'

"When he died," Becky continued, "the church in Meursault was jammed with humble people. I've heard he was a man who did a great deal for people, but insisted that it be done in total anonymity. He was very direct, very impressive, extremely out of the ordinary. And so is his daughter."

Lalou begins her day at 6:15 A.M., when she rises and does exercises while Marcel prepares breakfast. Domaine d'Auvenay is only four and a half miles from Auxey-Duresses, and Lalou is able to return to lunch with Marcel most days.

But on the weekends, it is different. Then, as often as is possible, Lalou and Marcel climb. On vacations, they climb. "We are so happy in the mountains," she says. "Today when we go to the mountains, all the climbers are young, perhaps twenty years old. Marcel and I are always the oldest. But I am a much better climber now than I was twenty-five years ago. In climbing, there is always progress."

And how does Perrine fit into this life? Perrine, the beautiful daughter and sweet-natured poet who, by the age of twenty-one years, had published two books of poetry.

"I believe Perrine has always been jealous of our mountain climbing. We started taking her skiing with us when she was seventeen months old. I used to hold her between my legs and ski with her like that all day. She learned to ski well. With climbing, it is different. She wanted to know why we didn't take her. But you can't climb when you are very young. Climbing takes strength, the kind of strength you don't have until you are perhaps fourteen, fifteen, sixteen years old.

"Perrine has other interests. She is at the university in Geneva. Her first book of poetry was published when she was sixteen and it sold out in six months. And yes, she is interested in wine."

Each fall, Lalou gives her Dégustation de Septembre. It is a private tasting held at her home and limited to fifty people, all that the three sitting rooms on the ground floor of her farmhouse can seat. For the most part, the guests are restaurateurs, mostly from France; importers from around the world; some wine people from other regions, particularly Bordeaux and Champagne; there are very few wives and even fewer wine writers. She organized her first September Tasting in 1966, and since 1971 she has held it almost every year, with the theme changing each year. In 1975, for example, she served thirty wines, five each from 1973, '71, '70, '64, '55 and '49; the game was to find the Auxey-Duresses in each year. In 1982, she called her theme "The song of our Burgundian soil in two vintages—1949 and 1959." In 1984, the year I attended, we tasted "A half century of Gevrey-Chambertin-Les Cazetiers and Mazis-Chambertin," a *Premier Cru* and *Grand Cru* respectively.

On a perfect day in the middle of September, those of us with the coveted invitations drove through the tree-lined driveway to the gravel courtyard in front of the old gray-stone farmhouse with its deep-teal shutters. We sipped apéritif wines as the family greeted us—elegant Lalou in a soft pink silk Chanel suit trimmed with black; pretty Perrine in a black pants suit; handsome Marcel in a dark blue suit. As the sun lowered in the sky, we were ushered into the house, where white vases of long-stemmed pink and coral roses filled the corners of the three rooms, and were seated at small tables covered with white cloths that fell to the floor. In the center of each table was a small vase of pink bud roses.

Men in black aprons and women in black-and-white uniforms —all employees of Maison Leroy—poured a total of thirty-two wines in six sets. The wines dated from 1983 to 1933, with each set moving back a decade. In each group of wines, we were told what we were to look for: identify the Gevrey-Chambertin-Les Cazetiers and their vintages; in another set, identify the Mazis-Chambertin 1955 and the Gevrey-Chambertin-Les Cazetiers 1955; and finally, in the last set, identify the Mazis-Chambertin 1933.

We worked diligently. We tasted and we filled out our score sheets, signed them and handed them in, rather like well-dressed, obedient students being given an examination in an exceptionally lovely classroom. But though we would all have liked to think of ourselves as at least advanced graduate students, if not full professors—and looking about the room, I could see some of the most famous and exalted people in the international wine world—when Madame Bize-Leroy read the correct answers, our scores, on the whole, were not exceptionally high.

"But it is not a matter of being able to identify every wine," a guest experienced in the events of the Dégustation de Septembre said. "We must think of it as a rare opportunity. How many people, even in this very knowledgeable wine crowd, have ever before had the opportunity to taste such a range of these two wines?"

Possibly only Lalou Bize-Leroy. Possibly only Lalou Bize-Leroy could have amassed such a collection. And possibly, too, only Lalou Bize-Leroy could have identified the wines. "She is an institution," the importer from the Netherlands said. "She is not trying to imitate anyone. But then, how could she? There is no one like her."

After the wine came the food—table after table of pâtés, roasts, smoked salmon, salads, meats and mousses, all as perfectly presented as the wine, the house, the family. Even the perfect star-bright sky seemed to have been ordered by Madame Bize-Leroy.

The next day, Lalou Bize-Leroy would be back in her office at Auxey-Duresses, tasting wine, as obsessed as ever with her dream of perfection. When the day was over, she would return to Auvenay, to "my adorable husband."

Criticism of Lalou Bize-Leroy is a recurring theme. She always leads with her chin, says one who has felt her sting. She is rich and so she can do whatever she wants. She makes impossible demands, says an importer.

Becky Wasserman sees her in a different light. "Lalou has always fought for what she believes in, and that is quality. Why is it no one is ever envious of mediocrity?"

21

ANDRÉ MUSSY:

AN OLD WINEMAKER'S TALE

André Mussy went to work in the vineyards in 1928, when he was fourteen years old. He is in his seventies now, a spare man of medium height with straight shoulders, white hair combed back, soft brown almond-shaped eyes and a face on which the skin, instead of following the downward path of gravity over the decades, seems to have tightened across his high, sharp cheekbones. He still works in the vineyards, although in a more limited capacity now that his cousin's twenty-seven-year-old son, Bernard, takes care of them. But he remains in charge of the cellar, making and finishing and bottling his wines.

With his wife, Mauricette, André Mussy lives in Pommard, in the house his parents bought. It is on the corner behind the *patisserie* that stands on the right side of the narrow Route d'Autun as you drive south through the village. Like many Burgundian *vignerons,* they have their home above their wine cellars.

André Mussy's family has been involved with wine for six, seven, perhaps eight generations, for so long, in fact, that he is not really sure. But he is sure of when the family began to buy its own vineyards.

"In November of 1856, here in Pommard," he said, showing me the fragile, yellowed deed. That first vineyard consisted of 47 ares (an are is 100 square meters), or just over an acre; it had cost 3,600 francs. Over the generations, his family added to the original purchase.

By the time young André Mussy began to work in the vineyards, the family had amassed about three-quarters of the nearly fifteen acres he now owns in Pommard, Volnay and Beaune.

By the time he himself was twenty-three years old, in 1937, he bought a parcel of the *Premier Cru* vineyard Pommard Les Épenots. "It is my favorite vineyard, my best," he says.

"I have sixty thousand vines, and at least three-quarters of them are old vines. The highest-quality wine comes from older vines. I have some that are sixty-three, sixty-four, sixty-five years old and still producing, but that is the maximum. The best comes when they are thirty to forty-five years of age. I replant when it becomes necessary, but it is very important to make the right selection of vines. The traditional *vigneron* conserves his older vines if they give good wine, and that is what I do. I use only grafts from the vines in my own vineyards for new plantings. And then, it is important to wait. For the first ten, twelve years, these new vines do not give quality. It is possible to choose vines that produce bigger quantities. But they may not make as good a wine."

We were sitting at the Mussy dining table, in a room whose dark furniture was decorated with carvings of grape clusters. On the wall was a crucifix and a photo of Pope John Paul II. Madame Mussy, a lively little dark-haired woman, not quite five feet tall, set out red-and-gold doilies shaped like vine leaves, and on them, blue-and-gold liqueur glasses. Into them Monsieur Mussy poured his Fleur des Raisins, a delicious *digestif.*

"When the grapevines are in flower in June, I cut the flowers and macerate them in aged wine for two to three months. Then I filter it, add sugar and blend it well. That's all. We don't sell it. It's my personal specialty, the liqueur de Monsieur Mussy. It's for us and our guests."

André Mussy began to estate-bottle some of his wine in the early 1950s. He still sells a portion of it in barrel to *négociants,* "from nothing to 50 percent; it depends on the year."

Those bottled under his own label, Domaine Mussy, are sold by Cannan & Wasserman. They include wines from the Beaune village appellation and two Beaune First Growths—Les Montremenots and Les Épenottes, both of which are situated along Beaune's border with Pommard; the First Growth Pommard Les Épenots, which lies close to the Beaune border; and the Volnay village appellation; as well as Bourgogne, Bourgogne Aligoté and Bourgogne Passetoutgrains. His estate-bottled production ranges from 5,000 to 22,000 bottles a year, depending on the vintage.

Things have changed, André Mussy says, in the more than half century that he has been growing grapes and making wine. But the major changes and the ones he feels are most terrible are those that have happened in the vineyards.

"In 1928, when I first went to work, there were no tractors, and only a few people—perhaps three or four in our village— had horses. We worked by hand. Gradually, when we could, we, too, bought horses.

"Generally, a horse begins to work in the vineyard when he is six years old and he continues until he is about eighteen. He is an intelligent animal and we worked together. A horse does not compare with a tractor. A horse's work is more refined, more careful and meticulous. The horse is man's friend. The tractor is only an iron machine, and man is the slave of that machine. When I worked with a horse all day, I was tired at night, but only physically tired. When I worked on a tractor, I was physically exhausted, but I also suffered from nervous exhaustion.

"For most of the year, I worked from about six in the morning to about six or seven in the evening, six days a week. In winter, we still have work to do in the vineyards—ripping out vines that need to be replaced, putting in posts, plowing, pruning. And I work in the cellar all through the year. Then, in the evening, I must work on my accounts and answer my clients' letters."

"It's not until 10 P.M. that he can think of me," Madame Mussy said, winking. "But by then, he is so tired. You know, I have never understood this work. I cannot understand how work can be the most important thing. Not the family or the home or your health. Nothing is more important than work. I suppose you must be born to it."

Mauricette was not born to the life of the vineyards. A native of Algeria, she met André Mussy when she came to Burgundy to visit her sister, who had married a man from Pommard.

André Mussy.

"In the old days," André Mussy said, "both husband and wife used to work together in the vineyards and the cellars. The wife would bring lunch to the vineyard. There was a small stone cabin in the middle of the vines and we would go there to eat. Not anymore. Now it's rare for a woman to work with her husband. Now everyone goes home for lunch."

When Mauricette and André were first married, she joined him in the vineyards. "For two years, she tried working with me," he recalled, "but she is a very tiny thing; she was not strong enough. In Algeria, she had been a secretary, and so we decided she would take care of the books and be our secretary instead. That was when we first decided to do some estate bottling."

It was after Mauricette "retired" from the vineyards that the Mussys' two children were born. First Serge, and later Odile.

Both children married when they were in their twenties. Serge had a daughter named Caroline, and Odile had a daughter named Stephanie. And in the tradition of Burgundy, Serge worked with his father.

"André had had three brothers," Madame Mussy told me. "Two died as children, and the other was killed in the war with Germany when he was twenty; that is why André inherited all the vineyards. There was no one else."

But André had his son, Serge, and he taught him what he knew—about how to care for the vines and how to make wine. "Except for electricity and some mechanical devices, I make wine almost exactly as my father and my grandfather did," André Mussy said.

One warm summer day in 1980, as Serge was working on the tractor in the vineyards of Pommard, he came to the end of a row and began to make a turn. The tractor hit a rock, went out of control and began to turn over. Serge tried to jump free, but he slipped and fell. At the age of thirty, Serge Mussy was killed, buried under a tractor.

In the living room of the Mussy home, where sun streams through a skylight onto dozens of begonia and bougainvillea and Christmas cactus, there are photos of both grandchildren, and in the adjoining room there is a framed photo of André Mussy holding his granddaughter Caroline. In the drawer of a small table, in a folder, are photos of Serge, and on one of my visits,

Mauricette took them out. As she was showing them to me, we heard André coming up the stairs. Quickly, the photos were shoved back in the drawer. He walked in the room and looked at her. "What's the matter?" She said nothing, just glanced at the drawer. He put his hands lightly on her shoulders. Then he turned away.

At harvest time, about twenty people come to pick in the Mussy vineyards. "Gypsies. The same families every year. Other *vignerons* use students and friends, but we prefer our nomads."

When the grapes are harvested, they are brought to the Mussy cellars. Monsieur Mussy has only one white wine—Aligoté—which is pressed immediately and fermented. The bulk of his work is with the reds.

"In the old days, we used to dump one basket of grapes into the vat at a time, then crush each layer with our feet. That meant we were using all the stems, and fermentation was much longer —twelve to fifteen days—and the wines were big and tannic. Stems give tannin, yes, but they also help to regulate the fermentation. If we destem, the berries break. If we do not destem, there are whole berries and that means a slower fermentation.

"Now I use only some stems. How much depends on the year. When the grapes are good, I use 10 to 15, maybe 25 percent. And this makes our fermentation shorter—usually seven to ten days, and most years, eight."

As a traditional Burgundian winemaker, André Mussy breaks the cap of skins, pips and stems that forms on the top of a vat of fermenting red wine the traditional way, by the *pigeage,* in which young men climb to the top of the open fermenters and tread the thick crust with their feet, just as Michel Lafarge does in neighboring Volnay. "Toward the end of the fermentation—the fifth or sixth day—there is the *grande pigeage,*" Monsieur Mussy says, "when the young men submerge their whole bodies into the vat of fermenting wine.

"The more you break the cap, the more color and flavors you get into the wine. To do this by pumping over lets too much oxygen into the wine and we lose flavors. Pumping over, in fact, lets in more oxygen than our open fermenters do. The best way to break the cap is with the foot. That's why we still use the *pigeage.*"

After fermentation, the red wines are put into casks and taken to the two deeper *caves* of the Mussy cellar. One was dug out of the sand and limestone that dominates this part of Pommard, in 1786; the other dates back over three hundred years. The wines remain there for about eighteen months.

When it is time to fine his wines, Monsieur Mussy does it the classic way—with fresh egg whites, four for each barrel, mixed with a very little bit of salt. "Salt helps to make the wine more brilliant. It is used often in Burgundy."

One day in May 1984, David Lett, of The Eyrie Vineyard in Oregon, Dominique and I were visiting André Mussy, tasting his wonderfully promising 1983 Les Épenots and Les Épenottes from cask.

"Usually, Pommard Épenots is bigger than Beaune Épenottes. But this Épenots was picked a day after it rained and it is a little lighter than usual," Monsieur Mussy explained.

But what interested him most that day was David Lett, the man who first planted Pinot Noir in Oregon. "What kind of rootstock do you use?" he asked David. "What other grape varieties do you plant? Do you need to irrigate? How do you prune?"

David answered his questions and then asked him one. "Would you like to come to Oregon to see?"

"Oh, yes, I would like that very much," André Mussy answered.

Before we left, Monsieur Mussy opened a bottle of Pommard Épenots 1979, made of vines planted in 1924. Still young and vibrant, and in need of maturing, it was a marvelous wine with great depth and a finish that lingered on lovingly.

"To make wine," Monsieur Mussy said, "your head must work as much as your hands.

"The older I get, the more I admire the generations before me. Look at what they did, look at the great wine they made— without college studies, without books, without modern equipment. This is a work of tradition. You must understand, I am not against modern technology. But to make wine, there is still nothing like an old winemaker with experience."

22

THE IMPORTER

AND

THE WINE MERCHANT

February in Burgundy is a time when dawn is often the color of dusk and days pass without a glimmer of sunshine. In the vineyards, the dark, gnarled vines are gaunt, and when a light snow falls, they stand in sharp profile against the white dusting on the ground. Workers, bundled against the raw cold, hunch over the vines to prune, tossing the cuttings into a *brouette à sarmenter,* a high-sided wheelbarrow in which the vine cuttings are burned. They flare up, for a moment's warmth, then wither into thin wisps of smoke. From stone houses, too, chimneys breathe out coils of smoke—thicker, steadier curls rising higher than those in the vineyards but, still, no less ephemeral. This is Burgundy's winter landscape.

While the outer world is at its most barren, the cellars are at their richest in February, which is why Barry Bassin comes to Burgundy then to buy wine. A New York City–based importer, Barry comes to France at least four, sometimes five times a year. He visits briefly in July or August or both months, and occasionally in September, depending on what the year's vintage promises to be.

"Does it look like it will be a big and popular crop? Or does it appear to be heading for a small crop that will create a shortage? I want to get the quickest pulse on it," he says.

In the fall, when he is in France to select his Beaujolais Nouveau toward the end of October or the beginning of November, Mr. Bassin makes the hour-long drive north to the Côte d'Or to get a first impression of Burgundy's new wine, some of which is still fermenting.

"I like to be there at the end of the growing season to talk to the man who raised the grapes, harvested them and is turning them into wine. I want to hear what he has to say about the health and condition of the fruit when it came in. Was there any rot, for example, and if so, how much? How did fermentation begin? Were there any problems or did it start easily? I find the *vigneron* in Burgundy tends to be very honest. He's talking to you as a farmer talking about his crops. I'm convinced no one can tell for sure how a wine will turn out by tasting it during fermentation, not even those of us who are trained as professional tasters. So the main purpose of my November visit is to talk to the *vigneron*. I need an indication from him on how that vintage will really be. From that, I make a fast decision as to whether I want to buy more of the previous vintage now or wait to order the current vintage.

"I'll give you an example. When I saw that the 1984 whites were commercially sound—and by that, I mean they are wines of the quality I want to handle—I did not order any more of the '83 whites. Among the '83s, the good will be extraordinary, but they will be relatively few. I cannot buy more '82 whites; they've already been sold. So, after getting a feeling for the '84s, I decided to wait for them to go on the market rather than look for '83s.

"On the other hand, let's suppose 1983 was a huge and very successful vintage for whites. If that were the case, I'd try to buy more of them and to sell all my '82s. But that was *not* the situation. We will have to wait for the '84s. So what I do is to tell my staff to sell the '82s mainly to those restaurateurs who are already carrying these wines on their lists. I feel committed to those people. There is not that much of the wine available, and so we don't try to place these wines with new accounts. We take care of our current customers."

A darkly attractive man with a wry smile, Barry Bassin was born in Washington, D.C. His grandfather was one of the first retailers to secure a wine and liquor license there after Prohibition's repeal, and of his seven children, five went into the wine and restaurant business. After four years in the air force, Barry went to work in the retail wine trade in Washington, until, in the early 1970s, he came to New York to head a pilot project for Schenley, which owns the wine company Dreyfus, Ashby. By the time he left Dreyfus, Ashby in December 1979, he was senior vice-president and national fine wines manager. A few days later, on the first business day of 1980, Barry opened his own firm, Barry Bassin, Inc. Only in his early forties, he has spent half his life in the wine trade.

February is Barry's "grand tour month" in France, when he travels through most of the country's wine regions—Alsace, Champagne, Bordeaux, Côtes du Rhône and the Loire—but he spends the greatest part of his time in Burgundy, the region he calls "my passion and my specialty."

When Barry arrived in Burgundy during the first week of February 1985, we began his cellar visits at Domaine Simon Bize in Savigny-lès-Beaune. Monsieur Bize's family have been vintners for five generations, and with his son Patrick's involvement, the Bizes can now claim six generations.

For each wine over a year old that Barry tasted, he wrote a detailed description. But not for the '84s. "With the new vintage, I'm interested in an overall impression. At this point, that's all I write down."

After Barry had tasted through the '84 and '83 reds (Savigny makes little white wine), Monsieur Bize asked him what else he would like to sample.

"My reserves," Barry answered. "All but one of these wines are already in the States," he told me, "but I like to taste them here to see how they compare with those I've tasted in New York."

About six o'clock, Monsieur Bize built a fire in the fireplace next to the tasting table. Madame Bize brought in sausage and crusty bread. And we finished the last of the wines—Savigny-lès-Beaune Guettes 1982, one of Barry's reserves and one of the lovelier, more complex Savigny wines I've tasted.

Barry Bassin buys wines from other regions of France, and from Italy, Spain and California, but he specializes in Burgundy, buying wines from Becky Wasserman and from Monsieur Bize, Aubert de Villaine and Domaine de la Romanée-Conti. He will also buy from the spot market, wines that "may be a good thing at the time. I have no relationship with the *vigneron* who made them, as I do with my other Burgundies, but they may be top-quality wines and I'll buy them as a one-time purchase."

How difficult is it to know in February after the harvest how a wine will be in a year or two or three?

"It's sometimes tricky. Some wines are voluptuous when they're young but will just not develop into interesting wines. Others are obvious in their youth," Barry said after our visit with Monsieur Bize. "I remember in 1976 the new white Burgundies were so charming and seductive that when I was tasting them in the cellar out of cask, I wanted to swallow—not spit—them.

"When you taste such wines, an alarm goes off and you imagine what they will be like in two, four, six years."

The next morning, we drove south to Bouzeron to taste Aubert de Villaine's 1984s, and later the three of us drove north to Vosne-Romanée, to Domaine de la Romanée-Conti, where Barry tasted both the 1984s and the 1983s in barrel.

We came out of the cellars with our fingers nearly as red as the wines and certainly as cold. "People always tell me how romantic my work is," Barry said, as we tried stamping some life back into our frost-numbed toes, "but a serious buying trip is hard, cold and sometimes painful. It reminds me of what my father used to say about his work. 'There are two wine trades—the one everyone thinks I'm in, and the one I'm really in.' Well, this is the one I'm really in—a day as cold as this and a cellar as cold and damp as the one we've just been in. I have to keep the wine in my mouth for a while just to warm it up to the point where I can get the fruit and flavors from it."

Then why come to Burgundy in February?

"Because by then I can taste intelligently. In November, I mainly listen to the *vigneron* and form a first impression. From then until February, the wine is still fermenting or it's going through malolactic or other processes. In February, I still listen to the *vigneron,* but I make my own decisions about the wine. If I wait much after February, the best wines are already sold."

That evening, in La Paillote, a Vietnamese restaurant in Beaune, Barry talked about buying wine.

"If there are any absolute rules, they are: One, go with the first impression; most mistakes are made when you change your

Barry Bassin tasting wines at Becky's farm.

mind. Two, never buy what you think the mass-market consumer will like; buy what you'd like to drink. And three, if you can't form an impression of a wine in a relatively short time, it's best to leave it. Otherwise, mind begins to take over intuition, and wine assessment is a matter of personal—not objective—appreciation."

Barry stayed on in Burgundy for another ten days, visiting and tasting with the Duc de Magenta, who lives in his ancestral château in Sully and owns, among other great properties, the domaine of L'Abbaye de Morgeot at Chassagne-Montrachet. Barry also visited Gérard Potel at Pousse d'Or in Volnay, Alain Burguet of Gevrey-Chambertin, Patrice Rion of Vosne-Romanée, and of course, Becky Wasserman and Dominique Lafon.

"I try not to make a definite decision at the moment I'm tasting, but I do try to give an honest appraisal to the grower," he said. "I believe he's entitled to that. Normally, I place an order before I leave Burgundy, but some years, that decision takes me longer than other years. For instance, the 1980 reds were not generally admired, but I liked them enormously. The vintage didn't have a good reputation, and I was a little nervous because they would be a hard sell. Still, I felt they were too good to be ignored. I thought about that for a while, because once I make a commitment to a grower, once I ask him to reserve a quantity for me, I always honor that reservation. I did finally post a reserve for them before I left Burgundy.

"I order directly from Domaine Simon Bize, from Aubert de Villaine and from Domaine de la Romanée-Conti. As for the wines Cannan & Wasserman represents, I always taste with the grower and order through Becky. If we order directly from a *vigneron* in substantial volume, we usually get the 10 percent that he would have paid a broker subtracted from our bill. But for me, Cannan & Wasserman is well worth that difference. Becky and Christopher take care of coordinating the shipping and the legal requirements, and they provide a liaison with the growers. Without them, I'd have to open offices in Burgundy and Bordeaux to get the services I get from them.

"And I respect Becky's expertise. I trust her opinion and her perspective. There are a lot of brokers in Burgundy. I think she's the best."

Barry usually returns to France in June, although on that trip he's likely to spend more time in Bordeaux than in Burgundy.

"Bordeaux is very different from Burgundy. It's more aristocratic. Everyone is extremely courteous, and entertaining is often lavish. In Bordeaux I taste with the cellarmaster and possibly with someone from the château involved in sales, but buying wine there is more like dealing in the stock market.

"In Burgundy, I taste in the cellar with the man who put the vine in the ground, tended it, picked the grapes and is nursing the wine to maturity. Burgundy is rustic, not aristocratic. It's intimate. When I buy wine in Burgundy, there's passion involved."

When the wines Barry orders arrive in the United States, he distributes them in New York and throughout other northeastern and mid-Atlantic states; as his young company grows, it is stretching its distribution channels farther westward into other major wine markets. Thus, from the *vigneron* through the broker to the importer, and then to the distributor, the wine finds its way to the wineshop shelf.

In Illinois, as in New York and most other states, a wineshop can order wines only through a licensed importer. After Pete Stern returned to Chicago from his trip to Burgundy, he placed an order for his shop, Connoisseur Wines, Ltd., not directly with Cannan & Wasserman or the other brokers with whom he deals, but with Direct Import Wine Co. in Elk Grove, Illinois. When I visited Pete at Connoisseur Wines, he was quick to point out his Burgundy section, the largest selection of fine estate-grown Burgundies I have seen in any wineshop in this country. "More than a third of my stock is in Burgundy," he said, smiling proudly.

The space that is now his shop on the corner of West Chestnut and Clark streets went through many former lives, including one as a tavern and another as a brothel, before Pete Stern transformed it into a wineshop. Unlike most wineshops, it has no large display windows. Instead, there are tall, narrow windows running across the side and slightly wider windows across the front of the shop, and except for the sign announcing its name and hours, and a peek through the windows, you would not readily expect to find a treasure trove of wine inside.

Looking through the Burgundy selection, I found four Gevrey-Chambertin producers whom Pete had chosen from the seven he visited when we met in Burgundy—Alain Burguet, René Leclerc, Georges Mugneret and Vadey Castagnier.

There, too, were the wines of Capron-Manieux, which we had tasted in Savigny-lès-Beaune, and those of Domaine Jacqueline Jayer. And there was a host of others sent to him via Becky Wasserman—the wines of Daniel Rion et Fils, of Hubert de Montille, Pousse d'Or, Pierre Morey, Denis Boussy, Jean Pierre Colin, Philippe Rossignol, Claude Cornu, André Mussy and Michel Lafarge.

It was a sunny Saturday in the spring of 1985, and people flocked into the shop. The tidy shop has other well-stocked selections—of Bordeaux, Côtes du Rhône, the Loire. But most of the regular patrons knew what they wanted. They headed for the Burgundies—red and white.

From the midst of this wondrous selection, Pete Stern picked up a bottle of Michel Lafarge's Volnay Clos des Chênes 1982. "You know, he's one of my favorite winemakers in Burgundy. I once remarked to him how amazed I was that he could make great wine year in and year out. His reply was 'Il le faut'—'I have to.' Sure, I said, but not many winemakers can do this in off years. He didn't say anything. He just shrugged. I guess he meant, 'I can only account for my own wines.' But what elegant drinking they make. They're masterpieces."

Three years after the vine awoke from its winter dormancy and flowered, nearly three years after the grapes had grown and were harvested and turned into wine, that wine was in the bottle and on the wine merchant's shelf, ready for the consumer to buy, drink and enjoy.

The last passage was completed.

Pete Stern holds a bottle of Lafarge wine in front of his wineshop in Chicago.

23

CONTINUITY

As the seasons move from spring to summer to autumn in Bouilland, so do the vegetables that Paul Gutigny pulls from the garden each day—salad greens in a multitude of varieties, asparagus, string beans, spinach, carrots, beets, peas, potatoes, onions, shallots. Strawberries and raspberries are part of the warmweather treats. So are cassis berries and plums.

The valley's hills are all luxuriance in summer, and colors take on new shades of intensity. There are greens flecked with gold and greens cooled with blue. The gray of the eastern cliffs sparkles with shimmers of white. There is a richness and at the same time a delicacy about the land.

In the fall, when amber and red begin to speckle the hillsides and the gold and silver light of summer softens, curls of smoke rise again from the chimneys of the stone houses. There are apples now, and walnuts. There are jams to be made and vegetables to freeze. Paul Gutigny butchers enough lambs to take the farm through the year, sells fifteen of the herd and keeps eighteen ewes for the next season.

And life at the farm goes on.

Sydney, who learned to turn a handle and open a door when he was a pup, still hasn't learned to close one.

Bertie, who finished his *stage* before 1984 ended, has graduated to the permanent staff and to the title of *attaché commerçial.* Early in 1985, he made his first business trip, to the United States, visiting Cannan & Wasserman clients in New York, Chicago, Atlanta, Detroit and other cities. A few months later, he

Dominique Lafon and Becky Wasserman enjoy a beer after a
session of wine tasting.

was on his second business trip as *attaché commerçial,* this time to London. After that, he started a series of study trips through France's other wine regions.

Other than that, he says, his duties haven't changed. "I do pretty much the same things I did as a *stagiaire,* only more of them, except that I no longer have to feed the dog and cat."

Dominique describes his job now as "second in command—sort of." Becky describes it as company manager. As Cannan & Wasserman expands, so do Dominique's responsibilities. He has made more business trips to the United States and more forays into the Côtes du Rhône, the Midi, Alsace, Champagne and Spain, sometimes with Becky and Christopher, sometimes alone, searching out new wines.

At the same time, he and his brother, Bruno, the second of René and Marie-Thérèse Lafon's four children, are taking over the management of the family's wine estate in Meursault. The vineyards, which have been under the *métayage* system, will revert slowly to the Lafons, so that by 1991, they will be totally under their control. Dominique has always worked in the domaine's harvest and made wine with his father; now he and Bruno are in complete control of winemaking operations.

After a six-month visit to Australia, Paul Wasserman is back, working in Burgundy. Peter Wasserman is there too, working on a documentary film about the medieval city of Autun.

And Becky? She continues to give a vibrancy to Bouilland. In this quiet valley, the time of day is measured as much by the neighbor's cows trekking past the farm to pasture in the morning, and back to their barn at dusk, as it is by the clock; and the light in the valley—strikingly brilliant in summer, a vaporous white mist during much of the year—marks the seasons as clearly as the calendar. As mistress of the farm, Becky adapts to the season.

As mistress of Le Serbet, her life keeps a steady pace throughout the year. There are trips to England and America and Spain, no matter what the month. And there are clients and wine friends who find their way to the farm at all times of the year.

In some ways, life has turned around. Becky rarely cooks now. But as her management skills have been honed by running Le Serbet, so have they developed in running the farm.

"What do I do that is completely separate from my work and the farm? I listen to music. And I read. I love to read. But I really have no friends who are not involved, or at least passionately interested, in wine. And I really don't take vacations.

"I'm content to be here. I love to curl up near the fire and read in winter, to be outdoors in the sun in summer. I'm lucky to be an American in France. I'm lucky to be part of two cultures. I am very much American in that I like clarity. But I think in French, in the bittersweet way that the French live life—in the past, the present, the future. Everything here takes time. Everything moves slowly. I can no longer imagine living anywhere but in Burgundy."

The circuitous path of her life that brought her to Bouilland stops at the entrance to the farm. It has led her home.

INDEX

Page numbers in italics refer to illustrations.

winemaking *(cont.)*
  pumping over in, 179
  racking in, 107, 108, 143, 168
  starter *(pied de cuve)* used in, 104
  stems used in, 104, 179
wine merchants, 6–7, 187–188
wines:
  acidity of, 104, 107
  barrel aging times for, 102, 107, 168
  bouquet of, 76, 82, 84
  cellar conditions for, 166–168, 170
  chaptalization of, 57–58
  filtration of, 108, 168
  fining of, 107–108, 168, 180

wines *(cont.)*
  longevity of, 169
  racking of, 107, 108, 143, 168
  shipping of, 142, 143
  tasting of, 75–76, 82–84, 184, 185
  terroir of, 58, 168, 169
  village and vineyard character evident in, 168–169
Winkler, Albert, 155
Winroth, Doreen, 118
Winroth, Jon, 17, 21, 116–118
wood-splitting industry, 25–26
World War II, 84

Yellowstone National Park, 20

ABOUT THE AUTHOR

Eunice Fried is a wine writer and lecturer and a frequent contributor to *Connoisseur* and the *New York Times*. Her articles on wine, food and travel have also appeared in *Harper's Bazaar, McCall's, Food & Wine, TWA Ambassador, American Way* and other publications.

Ms. Fried has lived in France and has traveled extensively through its wine regions as well as through those of other wine-producing countries.

She has served on innumerable wine-tasting panels and has been a judge in many of the country's leading wine competitions.